D1269293

10

THE CHURCH
IN THE
NEW LATIN AMERICA

Edited by JOHN J. CONSIDINE, M.M.

2

FIDES PUBLISHERS, INC.
NOTRE DAME, INDIANA

© Copyright: 1964, Fides Publishers, Inc.
Notre Dame, Indiana
Nihil Obstat: Louis J. Putz, C.S.C.
University of Notre Dame
Imprimatur: Leo A. Pursley, D.D.
Bishop of Fort Wayne-South Bend

Library of Congress Catalog Number: 64-8148

Prepared for publication under the sponsorship of the
CATHOLIC INTER-AMERICAN COOPERATION PROGRAM
(CICOP)
LATIN AMERICA BUREAU, N. C. W. C.

CONTENTS

Supplement
Latin America in Brief
A ready-reference summary of social and religious data
on each of the twenty Latin American nations.

Introduction

Probably the greatest single obstacle to friendly relations between Latin Americans and people in the United States is a mild but deeply built-in disdain on the part of the great preponderance of our citizens. Almost unconsciously the average American approaches the Latin American with the feeling that here is a man who comes from a part of the world where nobody knows how to run a government, nobody knows how to work a farm, nobody cares too much about overcoming illiteracy, illegitimacy, widespread indigence, and so forth.

However painful it is to dwell on this situation, it is salutary for responsible persons to face the problem frontally. The CICOP movement (the initials stand for Catholic Inter-American Cooperation Program) sets this as its goal. Its interest is to urge the conveyance of greater knowledge of Latin America, a better acquaintance with Latin Americans, and from this knowledge and acquaintance, greater understanding, appreciation, respect, mutual concern, joint achievement.

CONFERENCE LEADERS The 1964 CICOP conference was held in Chicago on January 20-21. Cardinal Cushing, as chairman of the United States Episcopal Committee for Latin America, called upon Archbishop Paul J. Hallinan to lead the meeting.

Archbishop Hallinan is chairman of the Sub-Committee on Cooperation which operates within the Bishops' Committee for Latin America of the national conference of the American hierarchy. His cooperators on the Sub-Committee are Archbishop Joseph T. McGucken of San Francisco and Bishop Coleman F. Carroll of Miami. Msgr. William J. Quinn of Chicago, Co-Director of the Latin America Bureau, N.C.W.C., was the conference director and Father Louis M.

INTRODUCTION

Colonnese of Davenport, Administrative Director of the
Latin America Bureau, was conference secretary.

The conference had six Cardinal Presidents, three of Latin
America and three of the United States. Those of Latin
America were Cardinals Quintero, Landazuri Ricketts and
Silva; of the United States, Cardinals Cushing, Meyer and
Ritter. Cardinal Albert Meyer of Chicago was conference host.

GREEN LIGHT FROM THE HOLY SEE   In addition to the blessing of Pope Paul VI for the CICOP conference, Cardinal
Cushing received from Cardinal Confalonieri, Prefect of the
Consistorial Congregation of the Roman Curia and President
of the Pontifical Commission for Latin America, a letter which
made it clear that the Holy See shared the conviction that the
purposes of CICOP represented immense possibilities for en-
during accomplishment.

THE GUESTS FROM LATIN AMERICA   Some 1,500 participants
gathered from throughout the United States, among them
representatives of the American hierarchy and the religious
communities of men and women and of the major activities
and lay organizations of the American Church.

The fifty guests from various nations of Latin America included distinguished religious and lay figures currently playing
important roles in the religious and civic life of their respective
countries. They included such authorities as Cardinal Silva of
Santiago; Bishop Manuel Larrain, President of CELAM (the
Latin American Bishops' Conference); Archbishop Helder
Camara of Recife, Brazil; Bishop Marcos G. McGrath of
Santiago de Veraguas, Panama; Bishop Jose Costa Campos
of Valenca, Brazil; Rev. Tiago Cloin, C.SS.R., General Sec-
retary of the Men's Conference of Religious in Brazil; Rev.
Renato Poblete, S.J., of Centro Bellarmino in Santiago; Abbe
Francois Houtart of Louvain and Bogota, Secretary-General
of the International Federation of Catholic Institutes of
Social and Socio-Religious Research (FERES); Rev. Jorge
Mejia, Editor of *Criterio,* Buenos Aires; Rev. Dr. Pedro

Velasquez, President, and Rev. Carlos Talavera, Sec-
retary, of the Inter-American Conference of Catholic Social
Action in Mexico; Dr. Aristides Calvani, School of Social
Science, Catholic University in Caracas; Senor Sergio Ossa
Pretot, Director of the Institute for Development of Chile.

It would be difficult to exaggerate the importance of this
contingent of Latin American participants. Their role was
indispensable for the success of the conference. At every
session, in every gathering throughout the day and evening,
it was their contribution which provided the essential conclusions, the requisite explanations and interpretations.

THE APPRECIATION OF GOVERNMENT OFFICERS   The CICOP
program is basically religio-social; certainly it is not political.
Yet it is worthy of note that its value toward the common
gocd was quickly recognized by major government officers.

At a public evening session on January 20, some 2,300
persons heard addresses by Senator Hubert Humphrey, Archbishop Miranda of Mexico City and Cardinal Cushing of
Boston on the theme *The New Image of Latin America*.
Through Senator Humphrey the conference received a message from Washington which recognized the human significance of the concern of the Catholic Church for Latin
America:

> The launching by the bishops of the United States of
> a ten-year program of assistance to Latin America, the
> Catholic Inter-American Cooperation Program, is a rec-
> ognition that the obligation to achieve social justice tran-
> scends national boundaries. It is recognition of an obliga-
> tion to seek what that great and good man Pope John
> XXIII called the "international common good." I am
> honored to have the opportunity to participate in the
> launching of this program.
>
> It was in 1961 that Pope John in his encyclical *Mater
> et Magistra* spelled out in bold new language the obliga-
> tion of nations that are rich and advanced toward those
> which are poor and underdeveloped. He stated:

"The solidarity which binds all men and makes them members of the same family requires political communities enjoying an abundance of material goods not to remain indifferent to those political communities whose citizens suffer from poverty, misery, and hunger, and who lack even the elementary rights of the human person.

"This is particularly true since, given the growing interdependence among the peoples of the earth, it is not possible to preserve lasting peace if glaring economic and social inequality among them persists. . . .

"We are all equally responsible for the undernourished peoples. Therefore, it is necessary to educate one's conscience to the sense of responsibility which weighs upon each and every one, especially upon those who are more blessed with this world's goods."

It was in that same year, 1961, that President Kennedy sounded the call for a new Alliance for Progress in this hemisphere. After ignoring our neighbors in this hemisphere, President Kennedy recognized that we could no longer ignore the revolutionary challenge of an unjust social order in the Latin American continent, could no longer ignore the shocking social and economic inequality between privileged and impoverished, between glittering capitals and festering slums, between booming industrial regions and primitive rural areas.

Senator Humphrey's interest in the program of the Catholic bishops is illustrated by the fact that on January 29 he described CICOP to the United States Senate as "destined to become an important instrument in promoting inter-American cooperation in the decades ahead." His address to the Conference was placed in the Congressional Record.

CICOP INTERNATIONAL AWARDS   A desire to envision matters in terms of a hemispheric horizon prevailed at the conference, as evidenced by the bestowal of the dual CICOP International Awards. Father Theodore McCarrick of the Archdiocese of New York, currently on the administrative staff of the Catholic University of America, chaired the CICOP

Awards Committee which chose President John F. Kennedy
posthumously as the 1964 recipient in North America and
former President of Colombia, Alberto Lleras Camargo, as
the recipient in Latin America.

The introductory chairmen for the conference were Msgr.
James Shannon, president of St. Thomas College, St. Paul,
Minnesota, and Msgr. Luigi Ligutti, delegate of the Holy See
to the Food and Agricultural Organization, Rome.

Msgr. Ligutti sounded an optimistic note:

> A most personal introduction on my part—Number
> one: I love Latin America. Number two: I am an optimist
> about Latin America. We have seen nations in the by-
> gone milleniums called to leadership in civilization after
> civilization, each successful to a greater or lesser degree.
> We may go back to Babylon, Egypt, Greece, Rome, Spain,
> Great Britain, and now the United States. A century from
> now, and perhaps less, it will be Latin America. The
> human resources of Latin America—and they come first
> —contain in themselves the greatest possibilities. There
> is the greatest potential, from a biological viewpoint, from
> a material viewpoint, from the viewpoint of Christian
> culture, that no other part of the world has possessed in
> like fashion thus far. In these possibilities there is no
> limit.

THE PRELATES FROM LATIN AMERICA   Archbishop Miranda
of Mexico City, with Archbishop Helder Camara of Recife,
Brazil, and Bishop Larrain of Talca, Chile, constituted the first
trio who as president and first and second vice-presidents of
CELAM headed the continental direction of Latin America's
episcopacy, now totaling some 540 bishops.

Archbishop Miranda recalled some recent history:

> Let us look at the new image. Years ago His Holiness
> Pope Pius XII, deeply concerned about the Church
> throughout the world, examined the Latin American
> countries. In 1955, he invited all our bishops to gather in
> Rio de Janeiro on the occasion of the International
> Eucharistic Congress. He sent us a magnificent apostolic

letter in which he gave us his thoughts regarding Latin America. He didn't partake of any pessimism about the future of Latin America.

All those who were privileged to be present (and this included the same three of us here today—Archbishop Helder Camara, Bishop Larrain and I) recognized that memorable reunion of two weeks as the most significant gathering in the whole history of Latin America. Out of it came the continental Episcopal Conference of Latin America which Pius XII instituted at our request. It was the very first permanent regional conference of bishops in the history of the Church.

We three bishops with you today were also present at another historic first: the meeting in Washington in 1959 of bishops from Latin America, Canada and the United States, to which Pope John XXIII sent Archbishop Samore as his representative. Out of Pope John's great interest came the efforts of our brothers in the United States, Canada, Spain, Germany, France, Ireland, England, Poland, Belgium, Italy, Austria. This is the real image, the fusion of zeal and love revealed through this practical working together for the future of the Church in Latin America.

This picture is being perfected by your meeting here. Looking to the future, through the second and third and each of your succeeding conferences, may you secure an ever better picture of Latin America.

Cardinal Silva of Santiago made this point:

I will tell you a true story. Years ago an 18-year-old boy was sent to me because he could not get along with his parents. I asked him what he thought was wrong. "Padre, when I was a little boy, my father and mother made themselves little with me and played with me like little boys and I was happy. But now I am grown up and my parents have remained little; they still want to play with me as if I were a little boy."

In Latin America many parents and priests, and sometimes your priests and your laymen when they come to work in Latin America, act with our laity as if they judged them still to be little boys. We shall build the Church in Latin America best if we treat our people like full-grown men and call upon them to carry burdens that grown-up men are proud to bear.

THE PROTESTANT OBSERVERS   Six Protestant observers were invited to the CICOP conference, and their reaction to the frank discussions was evidently one of admiring satisfaction.

Doctor Roswell Barnes, representing the World Council of Churches, described his reaction:

It wasn't long before I found myself in a kind of identification with what was going on here. I think this was first of all because of the real, genuine comradeship of the inter-personal relations, but even more because of what you were discussing and the way you were discussing it. I found that you were discussing the problems with which I am dealing in a different context and with a different group, most of them analogous to problems on our agendas.

The absence of spiritual complacency, or spiritual pride, has been a discipline to me . . . I'm reminded of what I've made almost a password around our offices recently: the statement of the Ecumenical Patriarch, when he met with the Pope in the Holy Land recently, that our only problems are theological. We still have theological problems and they are important, but to deal with them in the context of what is happening in the new day presents us with quite a new situation.

DOING SOMETHING ABOUT IT   The Papal program for Latin America certainly calls for practical action on as substantial a scale as the bishops of Christendom feel it advisable to request of their faithful. CICOP is basically an educational program, but as an integral part of the over-all Latin American effort of the Church in the United States it is logical that action should follow from our new-found appreciation of our fellow Christians below the Rio Grande.

The need for education on a parish level was emphasized by Msgr. Marvin Bordelon of Shreveport, Louisiana, at one of the CICOP sessions:

> Why do we not give proper consideration to communicating these urgent needs of Latin America through our parishes? There are currently 17,296 parishes in the United States. Is the Latin American problem going to remain merely a top level consideration, or is it going to get down to the grass roots of our people?
>
> As a pastor, I wonder if our various parish budgets do not reflect a great imbalance of interest. In our parish in Shreveport we spent last year 28 per cent of our total budget on capitalization of our parochial school. We spent 43 per cent on operating that same school. We spent 19 per cent of the total budget on the general needs of the people of God in the parish. Finally, 10 per cent of our income was spent on the deanery, the diocese, the national and international programs of our world Church. I question whether this 10 per cent reflects a sufficient catholicity of interest.
>
> My thoughts along this line were prompted recently when I learned that Broadmore Baptist Church in Shreveport, Louisiana, is giving thirty-three and a third per cent to extra-parochial projects, and some of its members lament that this figure does not reach 50 per cent.

A pastor in the environs of St. Cloud, Minnesota, offers an answer to Msgr. Bordelon's question.

A high school boy in his parish approached him recently. "I want to give this to one of our priests who is going to Latin America," he said, putting a wad of bills in the priest's hand. It was $125.

"Why are you doing this, son?" the pastor asked.

"Because I think it's so fine to help the people in Latin America who need priests."

The boy, his pastor explained, belongs to a family that works a small farm. He had earned this $125 over a period of more than a year by raising pigs and a couple of cows on his own. He had other plans for the money, but recent events in this diocese of farmers had changed his mind.

"It is astonishing," the pastor remarked, "what a flurry of excitement passed over the Diocese of St. Cloud when Bishop Bartholome announced that he was sending several of his priests to help the people in one of the dioceses in Venezuela. Everybody wanted to have a part in it."

Popular interest in Latin America has been growing among Catholics of the United States during the past several years. The recruitment of priests, Brothers and Sisters touches relatively few individuals. The call for lay volunteers involves many more persons, but it still affects only a small percentage of the total Catholic body. Thus participation by the great mass often is limited to bringing Latin America into one's prayer and into one's giving. The Catholic laity will reply with sacrifice if their leaders sound the call.

"Nobody," Pope John XXIII once declared in a message to the Food and Agricultural Organization, "can nowadays offer the excuse, in a world where distances count for nothing, that he is unaware of the needs of his far-away brother, or that it is not his job to help him. We are all collectively responsible for the undernourished."

CHAPTER I

Lessons of Yesterday for the New Latin America

A minor crisis arose a few hours before the CICOP conference was due to open in Chicago the morning of January 20, 1964. Bishop Marcos G. McGrath, C.S.C., then Auxiliary Bishop of Panama, had been detained in his home city. The riots over the flag controversy between Panama and the U.S.-controlled Canal Zone had proved so serious that it would have been a grave impropriety for the Bishop to leave his post.

Father Leo T. Mahon of the Archdiocese of Chicago who is pastor of San Miguelito, the parish in Panama City staffed by Chicago priests, came to the rescue by arriving with the Bishop's text.

"Sunday morning," explained Father Mahon to the CICOP delegates, "we buried the sixteen boys who were killed on the first nights and days of the rioting. A hundred thousand people were at the funeral. It was a very tense moment. The Bishop headed the procession in the three mile walk to the cemetery in the blazing sun.

"Then I returned with him to his work on this conference paper. He could easily, I think, have written a very fascinating paper on the crisis in Panama. It is a tribute to his profundity that he did not, because crises come and go in every country. As a fine theologian and good pastor he wanted to present you with something on a far bigger crisis, the crisis that is going on in the Church in this modern day.

"Imagine, then, Bishop McGrath—tall, young, very dynamic— sitting on top of the keg of powder in Panama as he wrote these pages."

THE PAUSE FOR PERSPECTIVE   Man, unlike purely spiritual beings, sees first the pieces of truth and must exert his reflective

1

powers if he would arrive at a whole view through effort, patience and spiritual concentration. We are often lazy, impatient or prone to rapid and nervous activism of a rather pragmatic kind; and so it is that the wholesome truths of life, death and eternity generally escape us except when they are rudely thrust upon our minds by crisis or by tragedy. So it is likewise that we can make the mistake of initiating and promoting vast programs of social action without taking pause to bring into the forefront of our thinking those several truths— whether historical, scientific, technical, social or religious— which we very well know to be not only valid but vital to the proper guidance of whatever program we intend to carry out.

WHERE THE CHURCH FITS   We are at present on the front edge of a great wave of inter-American cooperative action, both civic and religious, in which the Catholic Church of North and Latin America must perforce exercise a determining role in what is to come, in the properly religious sphere as well as in bringing about that dynamic motivation for a better social order without which no Alliance for Progress can move fast or far. This role of the Catholic Church in our hemisphere is an obvious truth which many enthusiasts of inter-American work would appear to ignore.

Although those of us here present would not share in this error, there are other errors which might be ours or, perhaps more accurately, there are other vital truths which, for lack of analysis, we fail to appreciate. It is worthwhile to probe into some of these truths. Chief among them are two considerations which are so obvious that it is painful to think how many embark upon Catholic aid to Latin America without giving them a glance, namely: "What do we know about Latin America, where it came from, where it is, where it is going?" and, secondly, "What is the role of the Church in Latin America?"

STRANGERS   The first truth we must recall in all its bald reality is that the United States and Latin America, in their civilization and cultures, have been foreign to one another since they began. This is a simple fact, but of broad significance. We should not be surprised that we do not know one another; we have had little occasion to do so. Even today the ordinary U.S. student learns much of European history, but almost nothing is taught him on secondary or university level about the nations and territories to the south. In Latin America, despite the present might of the United States, classroom history often gives the meagerest report of her past. A man conceives history in terms of his ancestors. The peoples of Latin America came mostly from southern Europe, those of North America predominantly from the north. We have grown off separate branches of a common trunk, and only now, by reason of economic and political necessity, only now in this century, and particularly since Franklin Delano Roosevelt, have we thought of ourselves effectively as neighbors, and possibly good neighbors and friends.

THE NEED FOR UNDERSTANDING   It is fine that we do so, and even urgently necessary. But friendship to be genuine and to be helpful supposes a knowledge of our friend. So-called friendship that is the fruit of religious or political expediency— for example, aid to Latin America while Communism threatens, or the lending of priests to relieve a present local shortage —does not outlive the expediency. The services it renders are unilateral because it does not make real contact at the other end; and the same services are conceived at home and exported intact without a sufficient feel for the "friend," his way of living, his way of thinking, the pattern of his problems.

A case in point would be the *a priori* determination of a United States Catholic that Latin American bishops should build up a parochial school system similar to that which the Church erected in this country. Such a determination would ignore the fact that this system in the United States originated in great part through a necessity which befell U.S. bishops to preserve the faith of immigrant Catholics in a Protestant culture. It ignores, too, the absolute impossibility of means (personnel and money) in Latin America for a massive effort which would attempt to draw millions and millions of children, rapidly multiplying, into parochial schools which do not yet exist. It is to ignore the fact that in many countries of Latin America the law provides, as it does for example in Germany, that religion be taught in the state schools.

SEEING THE CHURCH IN THE CONCRETE A more exact and true knowledge of the human situation of our Latin American neighbor will permit us to understand better his religious problems and perspectives. This brings us directly into our second question: the role of the Church in Latin America.

We must not judge the task of the Church merely in the abstract. Her mission in the world is unchanged and unchanging; but the world is constantly changing—partly by her doing —and so it is that the manner of her mission requires continual adaptation. If we are acutely aware of this fact we will not judge the action of the Church in Latin America in, let us say, the 19th century in terms of problems and situations which did not come into being until the mid-20th century; nor will we limit the Church's action now to the methods which were effective in the past. We should, in a word, be able to evaluate justly the action of the Church in Latin America in the period of the conquest, during colonial rule, throughout the republican era and at the present moment. There is a thread of continuity through it all: advantages and disadvantages which are created and passed on. There are also sharp changes, required by the times.

THE CHURCH'S MISSION TODAY Our catechisms are often deceptively pat in their description of the church's threefold mission to teach, to rule and to sanctify. Since the time of St. Robert Bellarmine, in reaction against Protestant rejection of external Church authority our manuals of theology and our catechisms have fixed their attention sometimes too exclusively on the visible aspects of the Church. (Take for example St. Robert Bellarmine's definition of the Church: "The society composed of men united among themselves by the communion of the same sacraments, under the jurisdiction of the legitimate pastors and above all of the Roman Pontiff" [De Ecclesia II-I].)

The Church is a mystery; it is an object of faith which we can only partially understand and which therefore, in the words of Pope Paul VI, "permits ever new and more profound inquiries into its nature" (Allocution to the Council Fathers, solemn inauguration of the Second Session of Vatican Council II, September 29, 1963).

GOD REACHING THE TEMPORAL   It is God who acts through Christ in His Church. Toward what end? Toward unity: the unity of all men in the love of God, in the unity of the living God. All born and yet unborn are to be incorporated into Christ: with Him they form the Church, they are the Church. He acts upon all, near and afar, through the invisible Spirit of God and through the visible ministry of His members. It is a "truly tremendous mystery," said Pope Pius XII, that we depend upon one another for our salvation. We are not saved singly but in society—in dependence on so many around us for all that we have, all that we know, all that we desire. In the Church we receive that spirit of love which will enable and bring to fruition all our single natures, desires and efforts. The Church is the instrument of Christ which would make us divine together with and in him; but it does so in the full social and historical context in which our salvation is to be wrought upon earth.

The Church as a religious society is distinct from the temporal order. Christian men, however, live deeply embedded in temporal order. Christ makes Himself present in each of these two manners: indirectly, through doctrine, and directly, through its personal and prudential application. In this area we run into many of the problems which have typified in one age or another the question of the Church and the temporal order: the problem of Church and State, of censorship and all forms of Church monitoring of morals, of collaboration between Churches for social welfare, of active toleration for all Churches, etc. We need only mention them here and point out how situations and human criteria over the centuries bring one or another problem to the fore. As in all matters of dynamic human relations, especially when complicated by the divine, an active balance is required.

A CLEAR APPRECIATION OF THE CHURCH   To plan the pastoral action of the Church, we must be clear on her nature and purpose—as clear as the mystery permits—especially when we would adapt her pastoral action to a radically different situation than was known by the theologians of past centuries. The Second Vatican Council set out for pastoral reform a thorough-going *aggiornamento*. It quickly found that this required a re-expression of the Church—in her mysterious inner life, in her members, in her episcopal constitution and in her sanctity and mission.

It is well to note how much we have grown in the last century in our appreciation of the Church. The function of the layman, his proper independence in the temporal order, his active participation in the liturgy and in the religious apostolate; the call of all Christians to sanctity; the community of all Christians around their bishops and the Supreme Pontiff—the visible reminders of Christ—in the one, living Mystical Body. These are all doctrines packed with power for a world desirous of ideals, of progress, of unity and of human well-being. The overflow of it all into the temporal order is envisaged already in the Council's Constitution on the Church, and will be made more explicit in the coming Constitution on the Church and the Modern World.

CHURCH REALIZATIONS IN LATIN AMERICA   Robert Ricard early in his classic entitled *The Spiritual Conquest of New Spain* (1492-1572) remarks that the first decades of Spanish occupation in the new world set the basis for social and religious patterns there for centuries to come. This remark is a valuable guide. We can divide the 472 years since Columbus's first voyage into four handy periods. It is the outline proposed by Father Egana, S.J., in his two-volume history of the Church in Spanish America, soon to be published (editorial BAC):

1. 1492-1566—the seeding period: the mud and thatched-roof Church.

2. 1566-1700 (from the accession of Philip II throughout the rule of the Hapsburgs)—period of consolidation: the age of cathedrals and universities.

3. 1700 (accession of Philip V, the first Bourbon) to 1815 —relaxation and decline. The Church's will is sapped by the decrepit state of Catholic thought in Europe, the rising mockery of the rationalists and the insistent pressure of the social revolutionaries against the order the Church had long known. The suppression of the Jesuits ruins many mission and educational centers across the continent.

4. 1815 (the independence of the various nations is assured) until the present—contemporary republican history. Throughout the 19th century the nations remain rural and aristocratic. Politics opposes the anti-clericals (liberals or radicals) and the conservatives in economic and social affairs. The issue is Church influence in all civil and social affairs—sometimes aggravated by the oposition of some bishops to the movements of independence. The Church suffers a serious collapse due to the protracted period in which bishops could not be named by the Holy See. Seminaries are closed or they significantly foreshorten their period of training.

Somewhere in the present century, a new period should be marked off in which characteristically the social problem becomes central—even to religious considerations. After the Second World War, this problem is greatly intensified and introduces the new epoch we now face.

THE PATTERN OF CENTURIES Looking back over these periods one is impressed by Ricard's remark. The stamp of medieval thought and social structure was placed upon Latin America and is still unmistakably there. For instance, the use of arms to spread the faith during the period of colonization was the same practice urged upon Charlemagne by Alcuin 700 years earlier. The Spanish universities provided resounding statements on the liberty of all men which the Crown supported in principle and many missionaries supported in practice; but the system of *"encomiendas"* rapidly set up the feudal land system still basic in many areas of Latin America. Other fundamental structural features imposed then are still found today. The close association of Church and State—though legally abolished in many nations—still dominates the thinking of many Latin American Catholics who look to the State for the solution of many religious problems which the State traditionally handled.

There is, then, an original stamp placed upon the Church in our Latin American regions; and this stamp remains engraved today, in greater or lesser degree, almost everywhere. Despite this fact of continuity, however, there are notable breaks, significant discontinuities. These likewise characterize the periods pointed out and briefly described.

An important criterion must govern our thinking: we must be slow to impose our judgments upon the past. The various discontinuities which separate us from the past make it difficult for us to adjust our thought patterns to what then must have seemed not only good but inevitable. There is much to admire in every period—more in some than in others. For example, the prodigious missionary efforts of the first religious missionaries—Franciscans, Mercedarians, Augustinians and Dominicans—are only matched by the adaptability of many of them (especially the Franciscans) to the mentality of their Indian catechumens. There is also much to regret in every period. And throughout all there is change; so that not everything that is good today would have been good in the past, nor is everything that was good yesterday adequate to the needs of today.

A SOCIETY WE MAY JUSTLY CALL "NEW"   So it is that the Church in each period is linked to the past and yet must emerge from it free from any encumbrance which would prevent her adaptation to the requirements of a new world. The Church faces today a Latin America that is rapidly changing into a society so different that we may justly call it "new."

There are many who predict that this new Latin America will abandon her Christian past entirely, in favor of a Communist structure. Others foretell, rather, a gentle sliding into a nearly universal agnosticism and the rejection of any moral code. We are far more optimistic; but we are at least sure that what does happen in Latin America depends largely on the Church —on us, on you, through whom our Lord has chosen to work in today's world.

CHAPTER II

Plagues That Followed Freedom

This chapter is the second of the two background studies which provide us with the setting for a theme (The Role of the Church in the New Latin America) that deals predominantly with the world of today. In it the combined contributions of Bishop Manuel Larrain Errazuriz of Talca, Chile, and Dr. Joseph A. Gagliano of Loyola University, Chicago, serve us well in understanding the major problems which confronted the Church at the end of the colonial rule and during the rise of newly independent republics.

We are told that Bishop Larrain, fine student though he is of Church teachings, would rather be known as a historian than a theologian. One of his fields is the French Revolution. He is currently President of the Episcopal Conference of Latin America (CELAM).

Doctor Gagliano is Assistant Professor of History at Loyola. He received his M.A. from Marquette University in 1956, while his Ph.D. in Latin American history was bestowed by Georgetown University in 1960. He is a member of the American Historical Association, the Catholic Historical Association, and the Conference on Latin American History. With his wife and their child he lives currently in Chicago.

THE FRENCH REVOLUTION AND LATIN AMERICA   This chapter concerns first of all the influence of that complex of ideas and events which we call "the French Revolution" on the religious life of Latin America. As Bishop Larrain assures us, we are guided not only by the curiosity of the historian who tries to analyze and understand the positive and negative forces at work even today in his field of apostolate. If we believe with Aristotle that "in order to know an object thoroughly we must study its origins," we grasp at once the importance of understanding the historical phenomenon of the French Revolution and discovering the imprints it has left on Latin America. This task is even more necessary because historians of our continent—perhaps carried away by the tendency to apply too easily the historical processes of the Old World to Latin American events—have often presented an unbalanced picture of the revolution as it affected Latin America.

The beginning of the 19th century was marked in Latin America by the independence of almost all the Spanish colonies, Cuba being an exception. The new countries each experienced a period characterized by many difficulties following the rapid rupture with the colonial regime. The Church likewise passed through a similarly difficult period.

To understand these difficulties it is very important to look at the general situation of the Church in Europe at that time. Events in Latin America were very much linked with the situation of the Church in Spain and Portugal and the rest of the European continent.

THE CHURCH AT THE END OF THE 18TH CENTURY   During the 18th century in Europe, there was a progressive deterioration of relations between Church and State. During the Middle Ages, all society had been integrated by a Church-dominated religious and intellectual culture. This universalism had taken the form of an ecclesiastical and political power dependent on the papacy. Little by little, however, the idea of the autonomy of the State was born—due to result in progressively increasing domination of the Church by the State. This development was accentuated by the trend toward absolutism. In Spain it was exemplified by the Caesaropapism of Philip II; in France by the triumph of Gallicanism under Louis XIV.

This situation had great influence on the Church in Latin America. Following the discovery of the continent, the Pope had given to the Crown of Spain the right of patronage,* which proved to be at the same time both a protection and a source of oppression for the Church. During the period of colonization the Spanish monarchs increased their power over the Church. In the beginning they sent missionaries and materially helped the work of evangelization, but they rapidly began to assume other roles as well. They even made decisions on the expulsion of priests, on ecclesiastical nominations, on the interdiction of the publication of religious documents including pastoral letters. The *patronato* came to be conceived as a royal right and not as a privilege granted by the Holy See.

DEVELOPMENT OF NEW IDEOLOGIES   The 18th century had witnessed the development of a new philosophy—that of the Enlightment—which among other things rejected Revelation. It meant the adoption of a kind of deism or even atheism. These trends of thought expanded rapidly in France and in all Europe through a truly great literature developed by Voltaire, the Encyclopedists, Jean-Jacques Rousseau, and similar powerful voices. It took the form of anti-religious aggressiveness especially against the Catholic Church.

Bishop Larrain notes that this spirit exercised an influence beyond the limits of Europe. In the United States, the Constitution of 1787 was based on the separation of Church and State. This was surely the result of the new ideology. As it turned out, it proved a protection for the Church because it assured liberty of worship. It served as a legal form of religious tolerance. In Latin America the situation was different. The only organized religious body was the Catholic Church, and the new ideology played especially against her.

———————

* *Patronato* (Portugese: *Padroado*)—The complex of concessions made, during the early years of the so-called "Age of Discovery," by the Holy See to the sovereigns of Spain and Portugal, giving the crown the right and consequent duty of establishing the Church in the new lands. Among the concessions granted the Crown was the privilege of presenting three candidates for each major ecclesiastical post, one of whom was to be named to the office by the Holy See.

True, long before these new ideas reached Latin America with their special theories on the social contract, democracy, liberty and equality, a number of Creole* generations had been trained in the thought of the Spanish Scholastics, who developed the doctrine of the origin of civil power and of the limitation of its practice. Both in the schools of philosophy and in private libraries, the works of Vitoria, Francisco Suarez and Luis de Molina were found and discussed. These works assert—contrary to the official theory of the divine and unlimited right of kings—the traditional teaching on the participation of the people in the creation of power, the ethical limitation of power, and the repudiation of tyranny. These theories, which had caused the expulsion of the Jesuits, were impressed on the minds of the Creoles and constituted the main ideas which justified the revolution for independence.

SEPARATION OF CHURCH AND STATE   The French Revolution was not only a major event in the history of the Church in France, but in all other European countries as well. It meant the destruction of medieval institutions and created for the Church a completely new situation. But the transition from the medieval to the modern has not been realized without problems.

The conflict between the Revolution and the Church was not only the consequence of social and political factors. New tendencies in philosophical, political and religious points of view were involved. The conflict resulted in violent anticlericalism and even in persecutions. In Central Europe the revolution gave rise to new constitutional states, with separation of Church and State. It provoked the loss of the Papal territories at the end of the 19th century and the crisis between Italy and the Vatican, solved only in 1929.

In Latin America the movement for independence at the beginning of the 19th century had close relation to the revolu-

---

* Persons of Spanish descent born in Latin America.

tionary movement in Europe. The religious problems in Latin America were intimately related to those stirred up by the French Revolution, even though the basic aims in Latin America were to oust Spain and its colonial administration. After independence the relations between Church and State were established on a completely new level.

In Latin America the anti-religious spirit of Europe's philosophical movements also had great influence. Not only were traditional privileges abolished, but many other measures were taken to curb the position of the Church.

THE HERITAGE OF LAICISM   The most characteristic phe-nomenon inherited from the Revolution was laicism. This was the banner of the parties which little by little came into exist-ence in the last century. Tolerance was their key doctrine, but their followers invented a civil religion characterized by an in-tolerance which preyed upon Latin American Catholicism. Laicism was a naturalistic religion, without dogmas, which assumed a different character in each one of its followers. All concurred, however, in their strong desire to snatch from the Catholic Church, one by one, the prerogatives which allowed her to bring religion into public life. The aim was to confine her to the sacristy.

The most important bastion behind which laicism became strong was education. It became obligatory (a good thing), but laicist. In the best of cases, religious instruction became a matter of free choice in public schools. However, in some countries, at least during certain periods, it was totally elim-inated. The Church was denied its right to teach religion to Catholic children. Though the old system perdured whereby the State paid the ecclesiastical ministers, the State often put incredible pressures upon the clergy to lessen their prestige and effectiveness among the people.

THE STRUGGLE FOR A NEW HIERARCHY   With the coming of independence, the continent counted six archdioceses and 38 dioceses. Even if this number had been sufficient during the colonial period it was so no longer, in view of the division of the continent into a number of new countries. The majority of the pre-independence bishops had ruled Metropolitan Sees. These bishops had left or had been expelled or had died without being replaced.

However much disaster this caused the Church, Dr. Gagliano feels it is very important for us to understand the great effort that was made to overcome the impasses that brought about this situation. The simplest assertion that independence resulted in a Church without a hierarchy ignores the many years of extremely complex diplomacy between the emerging nations of Latin America and the Holy See. The insurgents wanted papal recognition not only to facilitate the acceptance of their states in the community of nations but to maintain continuity in the hierarchy. Several factors militated against an easy transition in the Latin American hierarchy. The papal diplomacy of Spain was directed against any recognition of the emerging nations. The revolutionaries demanded that the Spanish hierarchy in the New World be replaced by Latin Americans or at least bishops who were not opposed to their national aspirations.

While Spain had insisted that changes in the hierarchy were subject to crown approval, the insurgents contended that the *patronato*, which the Crown had enjoyed for three centuries, was transmitted to the newly independent States as an integral part of their national sovereignty. The papacy, however, regarded the Wars of Independence as an oportunity to eliminate the *patronato*, and maintained that it was a privilege granted solely to the Spanish Crown which ended when the Americans separated themselves from regal authority.

The prolonged and complex negotiations, coupled with the disruption of communications between the Holy See and the hierarchy, had an adverse effect on spiritual life in the New World. In Colombia, no less than six sees fell vacant. By 1829, there was not a single bishop left in Mexico. Eventually heeding the admonitions of Cardinal Consalvi that unless the Church settlement were reached soon, a schism might arise in the New

World and Americans would be exposed to "Methodists, Presbyterians, and even sunworshippers," Leo XII decided to restore the hierarchy in Latin America, leaving the issue of patronage for subsequent concordats with the new nations. In 1827 he preconized the candidates presented by Colombia as proprietary bishops. Between 1827 and 1836, similar papal agreements with the other nations filled the vacancies which had arisen in the hierarchy during the independence period.

POLITICAL ASSUMPTION OF CHURCH AUTHORITY   The failure to establish concordats clarifying the question of national patronage caused the Church numerous difficulties. One of the most serious problems, notes Dr. Gagliano, was the threat of Caesaropapism in those nations where dictatorships emerged. Even in Brazil, however, during the turbulent period of Regency, Diego Feijo, a liberal priest who served as regent, proposed and supported projects to nationalize the Church, establish a married clergy, and make doctrines subject to Brazilian modification. Gabriel Garcia Moreno, whom critics accused of creating a theocracy in Ecuador, often dictated to the hierarchy and attempted to use the Church as an instrument to perpetuate political conservatism. In Venezuela the hierarchy became the victim of the personalism of Antonio Guzman Blanco.

Nowhere was Caesaropapism so fully realized in the post-independent period, however, as in Paraguay during the long dictatorship of Jose Gaspar Rodriguez de Francia. Unlike other revolutionary leaders de Francia never welcomed the recognition of the papacy. He appointed one of his own creatures as archbishop of Asuncion. Among his church reforms were the expulsion of regular clergy who refused secularization, state confiscation of church properties, and the closing of the sole theological college in Paraguay so as to prevent the future training of priests. The demoralizing effects of his long rule were not appreciably checked until after the tragic War of the Triple Alliance. Between 1881 and 1911, only sixty priests were graduated from the revived seminary in Asuncion,

the only institution for the training of the clergy. Almost a
century after the Francia Era, there were less than 100 priests
in Paraguay to serve a Catholic population of approximately
1,000,000.

THE CHURCH A TARGET OF POLITICS   In addition to the threat
of Caesaropapism, the hierarchy was confronted with other
attempts to alter the role of the Church in society. Opposing
views on the position of the Church became, in fact, a basic
source of conflict between the emerging conservative and
liberal political parties. Much of the 19th century history of
Colombia and Mexico was concerned with the struggle over
clericalism. The liberals viewed the Church as a principal obstacle to national progress and reform. With their tendency to
oversimplify deeply rooted socio-economic problems, they contended that all evils would disappear if Church and State were
separated, the extensive properties of the Church secularized,
and its control of education ended.

The conservatives regarded the Church as an essential institution for the maintenance of continuity and stability in the
social order. They often supported alteration of the Church's
exclusive position, however, so as to stimulate immigration or
economic expansion. Diego Portales, for example, while up-
holding the 1833 constitution which proclaimed Catholicism as
the religion of Chile, insisted that earlier concessions granted
to Anglicans be retained so as to maintain favorable commercial relations with English traders.

Regarding the liberals as a menace to the independence
and economic security of the Church, the hierarchy, Dr.
Gagliano explains, saw no alternative to formation of an
alliance with the conservatives in the political battles of the
19th century. Several examples can be used to illustrate this
alliance. In Mexico, when Valentin Gomez Farias began an
anti-clerical reform in 1833, the heirarchy supported a conservative rebellion which forced him into exile and revoked
his legislation. The alliance was maintained during the Reform Era of Benito Juarez so as to restore ecclesiastical

courts and Church properties. The heirarchy subsequently supported Porfirio Diaz, who permitted a restoration of the Church in return for financial and political assistance. Although the Church apparently enjoyed a significant revival, the hierarchy became regarded as an instrument of "Diazpotism." Opposition to the religious and social policies of Bernardo O'Higgins contributed to an alliance between the Chilean hierarchy and the oligarchy of great landholders and merchants. The hierarchy would be viewed as the partner of this oligarchy until relatively recent times. When Bernardino Rivadavia attempted to diminish the influence of the Church in Buenos Aires, the clergy gave its suport to the Federalists. The subsequent alliance with Juan Manuel Rosas served to identify the hierarchy as the submissive tool of the Rosas tyranny. He openly dictated to the Church through Mariano Medrano, the pliable Archbishop of Buenos Aires.

THE NEED FOR CHURCH REFORM   Preoccupied with political disputes, the hierarchy did not, and perhaps could not, often adequately concern itself with the problem of Church reform. The need for reform preceded the independence period, but it became increasingly urgent following the turbulent and disruptive years of revolution. The question of clerical reform was a political issue. In 1831, for example, Francisco Vasquez, with papal approval, proposed the reform of religious houses in Mexico. His efforts were impeded, however, by a coalition of liberals and radical priests who demanded abolition rather than the reform of religious communities.

The need for clerical reform was recognized during the post-independence period. Garcia Moreno, notes Dr. Gagliano, devoted much of his political career to personal direction of the reform of the clergy in Ecuador. A recent study of *latifundismo* in 19th century Mexico reveals that the parish priest of a hacienda in Coahuila received fees ranging from five to fifteen pesos for administering various sacraments. The average monthly wage of laborers on this hacienda was five pesos. Although the observations of travelers sometimes lacked objectivity, they reflected the more serious shortcomings of the clergy. In her sentimental novel *Aves sin Nido*, Clorinda Matto de Turner described the clergy of the Peruvian Sierra as the exploiters of the downtrodden cholos and Indians. The same charge could be leveled against many of the Bolivian clergy during the post-independence period.

Corruption is cited as a contributing factor in the failure to develop native vocations in many Latin American nations. The shortage was substantial even in the stronger nations such as Mexico and Argentina. Various nations long before our day invited European religious to establish schools and charitable institutions in their countries. The influx of foreign clergy, however, never was adequate to offset the absence of native vocations in Latin America.

DISAFFECTION OF THE INTELLIGENTSIA   The disaffection of the intelligentsia was another significant problem confronting the Church during the post-independence period. Although some hostility existed before independence, during the Revolutionary period the intellectuals turned more often to the political philosophy of St. Thomas Aquinas than to the contractual theories of the *Philosophes* for justification of separation from Spain. Following independence, however, they seldom demonstrated a continuity of Catholic thought in their political and social orientation. Instead they sought guidance in various materialistic philosophies—for example, the utilitarianism of Jeremy Bentham profoundly influenced intellectuals in Argentina, Brazil, Chile and Mexico during the early national period. Subsequently, the *Cientificos* of Mexico and Guatemala, as well as intellectuals in Brazil and various other nations, sought solutions to their national problems in the positivism of Auguste Comte.

ABSENCE OF A SOCIAL PROGRAM   Simultaneously, during the post-independence period, the church lost its identity as the champion of social justice. Although the Church's concern with social questions in Latin America may seem to be of recent origin, missionaries in Santo Domingo, as early as 1510, defended the rights of the Indians. Much of the social legislation during the conquest, ranging from the abolition of Indian slavery to the payment of just wages, resulted from demands of missionaries and bishops such as Bartolome de las Casas. Although the clergy seemed less committed to social questions during the waning days of the colonial period, Hidalgo's revolution in 1810 was perhaps more social than political in character. Following the alliance with the conservatives during the post-independence period, however, the hierarchy often regarded social reform as part of a liberal plot to despoil the Church. Even in those nations where the Church was secure, the hierarchy played no role in the quest for social reform. In Chile, for example, the hierarchy condemned the Utopian Socialism of Francisco Bilboa and the Marxism of later radicals, but it proposed no positive program to improve the conditions of the lower classes. In view of the profound upheaval in Latin America during the present century, the loss of its identity as the champion of social justice has been among the most unfortunate consequences for the Church.

THE PROGRAM OF RENEWAL   In the immense task of renewal which Latin American Catholicism is facing today, Bishop Larrain assures us that the Church is prepared to look at reality without fear. The heritage of the past—the typically Latin American way in which it solved its problems—should guide the Church in its desire for renewal in order to keep intact the deeper values and leave aside what is accidental.

This is an undertaking which requires adaptability and imaginative thought. With promising creativeness the Church in Latin America looks toward the future, observing the signs of the times in order to discover the direction which Providence wishes to give to her development. Her leaders have already set about the positive tasks they must accomplish in the spirit of the Ecumenical Council.

CHAPTER III

The Great Resurgence in Today's Latin America

Thus far we have dwelt on the past. Now we ask where the Church stands in the rapidly changing Latin American society of today. We are looking for no litany of sweet nothings but, rather, a down-to-earth appraisal of where both Church and society are directed.

We are provided with what we are searching for by an able study from the pen of Father Renato Poblete, a Chilean Jesuit well prepared to meet this need. Father Poblete specialized in sociology at Fordham University and on returning to Chile became the director of the Centro Bellarmino. He has contributed in a major degree to the socio-economic study of a group of specialists who have worked with Father Roger Vekemans, S.J., of Belgium, a project which provides a continental pattern for Churchmen and technicians called upon to meet the rapid social evolution of our times.

THE OLD ACCEPTS THE NEW   To anyone who has been interested in Latin America, it is obvious that the Church was present in the making of the culture of our continent. The Church was incarnated in almost all human activities. Since the first years of colonial times, the priests not only fostered the cultural aspect of life, with schools for the Spaniards and for the children of the Indian chiefs, but they also built canals for irrigation, brought from Europe new seeds for better crops, and taught craft skills to the people. The Church was aware of the abuses of the colonists and tried to defend the Indians, or at least to obtain better legislation for their protection. All these activities were maintained almost like a monopoly until the period of Independence. The Church was so involved in all human activities that we can say there was a sort of Christian society, a time of *cristiandad*.

This traditional, and basically feudal, society has left some deep signs in the rural world, where a great majority of the population remains on the margin of social, political, economic, and cultural life, thus experiencing only recently a process of change.

The mission of the Church cannot prescind from the socio-economic structure of the world in which she tries to become incarnate. That is why we have to know these elements in order to understand the action of the Church.

A WORLD MARKED BY CHANGE   The characteristic of the new Latin American world is *change*. First of all, there is an extremely rapid growth of population. Population figures have risen from 63 million in 1900 to 100 million in 1924; 163 million in 1950; and to more than 200 million today. This quantitative growth implies a tremendous change—a total and rapid change which has affected all human social structures and all human activities. Demographic distribution of the population has also changed a predominantly rural society to an urban one. In 1945, 39% of the population was considered urban; today over 50% is now living in the cities.

Obviously we are facing a rapid urbanization, with an extremely disproportionate growth of some cities in each nation. We are entering into a technical civilization with a progressive integration of the marginal masses into the social life, a change that is now affecting the rural society, as a result of the penetration of mass media of communication and new roads into these areas.

New social classes are emerging: the working class and the middle class.

We are witnessing the birth of new institutions, new social movements, new political activities. These transformations of society, we know, are not only Latin American phenomena, but are part of the progress that we observe in all modern life.

But one of the characteristics of our Latin American continent is that although all the advantages of technical civilization have reached Latin America, they are benefiting only a small and select group. The large majority have only aspirations, plus a consciousness of the tremendous contrast between their own situations and what they see they should have.

THE CHURCH'S UNFAVORABLE POSITION   We know that the Church carries its message through existing social structures. For this reason, the Church is also affected by this social change. The Church faces this social change in a very unfavorable structural situation.

There is today about one priest in Latin America for every 5,700 persons, with a range that goes from 3,000, as in Colombia, to 12,000 in Guatemala. In spite of the considerable effort made in Latin America as well as abroad, the demographic explosion surpasses any expectations we may have of maintaining this proportion. Thus, for example, in the last five years the increase of the Latin American population has been twice that of priests and seminarians. In the last fifteen years we have had an increase of 12,000 priests, but the population has grown more than 50 million during the same period.

This situation has important consequences for all religious institutions. The traditional pastoral structures, such as the parish, being so unwieldy, do not respond any more to the religious needs of the daily life of the people and must undergo a change. This must imply greater adaptability and decentralization. Parochial structure has to be seen in relation to the area, density, methods utilized, and so forth. The area fluctuates between 100 and 600 square miles and the average parochial population varies between 10,000, as in Colombia, and 35,000, as in the Dominican Republic. Moreover, it is not hard to find cities with an average of over 50,000 inhabitants per parish.

INADEQUACY OF OUR TEACHING APPARATUS   It is not enough to present this structural problem only with numbers. We have to see what has happened to the means at our disposal for evangelization. It is not enough to say that Latin American Catholicism is more than four centuries old. Tradition in this case is not sufficiently decisive to communicate by itself values, attitudes, and norms. There are people involved; a sustained action is necessary to communicate Christianity.

The channels we have used in the past to transmit the fundamental ideas of Christianity have suffered deep social and cultural changes. In the past the transmission of the divine message was easily accomplished, since we lived in a relatively unchanging monoculture, which generally facilitates and reinforces the transmission of ideas. There were many institutions, like the family, school, and parish, that reinforced the doctrine preached by the priest.

THE NEW SOCIAL PATTERN   Further, social control, which helps not only the transmission of ideas but also the maintenance of a certain stability in patterns of behavior, was in times past extremely helpful in many ways. Authority was another element in this kind of society to facilitate the transmission of ideas.

But today we live in a different world. We can find now in almost all the areas of Latin America, in varying degrees, a pluralistic society. There is not just one set of norms, values, attitudes and opinions; there are different values and norms emanating from secularism, Communism, and other sources. The intermediate groups, like the school, family and parish, do not reinforce the same doctrines, but oftentimes are in competition, opposing the ideas that were communicated to them by the Church.

Furthermore, social pressure is not as strong today as in the past. Living now in a more democratic society, we find that authority is continually being questioned. Therefore, a more personal commitment is needed, and we cannot count on the traditional way of transmitting the Word of God.

NEW AIDS NEEDED FOR PARISH LIFE   To summarize briefly: at one time religious tradition could be maintained because of the rigidity of the fundamental social structure and the fact that, basically, social structures were identified with religious structures. In spite of the lack of priests, anti-clericalism, etc., the population then remained basically Catholic. But today these structures are no longer identified. Therefore we have to recognize that we live in a pluralistic society, but unfortunately we are still using in many cases methods of evangelization proper to a monocultural society. The mythical aspects of rural, traditional Catholicism do not respond any more to the new values developed by a technical civilization. Religious rites are void of their content and have no personal meaning for the people, since the use of Latin has made the transmission of fundamental religious values difficult. The search for community, so characteristic of our days, is not in accord with the large formal structures of parish life.

CURRENT RELIGIOUS ALLEGIANCE   What is, therefore, the religious situation of Latin America? To present this we can analyze some indices of religiosity. First, there is religious affiliation as expressed in the national census. The most elementary step in church affiliation is to say one is a Catholic. In the national census such declaration varies from 65 per cent in Uruguay to 98 per cent in Colombia and Peru. Such declarations might prompt some to talk of Latin America as a Catholic continent.

Mass attendance implies a sense of belonging and participation stronger than the mere response to the national census. There we can find a statistical number that varies much from rural to urban religious practice and from one socio-economic group to another. In some worker areas in big cities, we have from one to three per cent of adult Mass attendance. In some of the middle and upper-class parishes, attendance at Sunday Mass goes up to thirty per cent. This index of religiosity has not at all the same meaning that it has in the United States, because problems like lack of priests, long distances, and the misery of the people make Mass attendance difficult.

The migration to the cities (Lima receives 1,000 Indians from the highlands daily) shows that people coming from areas where they were accustomed to see a priest once a year cannot begin the practice of weekly attendance at Mass right away. A sense of responsibility for fulfillment of this precept is very vague among people who traditionally have been accustomed to demonstrate their religious sentiments and attachment to the Church in other ways.

THE TELLTALE ABSENCE OF VOCATIONS   Priestly vocations are also a sign of religiosity; and here we can see that, with the exception of countries like Colombia, the number of semi-narians and newly ordained priests is smaller than the natural growth of the population. It is due only to the help of foreign priests that we have been able in some countries to keep the same proportion, inadequate as it is. Some places, like the Archdiocese of Santiago, Chile, have exactly the same number of diocesan priests as in 1925, when the population was only one-third of what it is today and the problems were simpler.

The lack of clergy, the size of the religious structure, and the failure to work together with laymen explain the religious ignorance that one may find in different degrees in all the social groups. This also explains the superstitions, spiritism, which is a sort of religious syncretism, and other religious deviations.

PROSPECT OF INCREASING DIFFICULTIES   It is important to be aware of the situation that will become worse in the future unless there are some radical changes in the apostolic work of the Church. The projection of population growth tells us that in a period of twelve years we will have 100 million new inhabitants to Christianize. The proportion of priests in the most optimistic forecasts will be even smaller than today. Another aggravating fact is that in the future, society will rapidly lose its traditional aspect and all will be exposed to a large variety of ideologies. This means that we have to insist constantly on a more personal commitment to the faith, rather than count too much on mere tradition to carry on the message of Christ.

BRIGHT SIGNS OF HOPE   At this juncture, one might be inclined to think that Latin American Catholicism will repeat the old, sad story of death and extinction as witnessed by the North African Christian communities of centuries ago. But there are brilliant signs of a dawn of hope. In some of the Latin American countries the Church, even anticipating the wishes of the Ecumenical Council, has had the courage to face reality and to evaluate its shortcomings, however hard and painful this might be.

This search for the truth, this analysis of our previous modes of acting without being afraid to recognize our mistakes, is really a most healthful sign of vitality. This knowledge is basic for planning the action of the Church in a more realistic way. In these countries the goals that we have to obtain have been studied and the priorities of means have been fixed according to accepted criteria. This may sound a little prosaic, but as a matter of fact shortly before he died Pope John XXIII asked all the countries of Latin America to undertake this task of planning.

Planning, which leads to a greater effectiveness in the action of the Church is obtained by using resources in the best possible way. Planning means, too, that in many cases the Church decides against doing things the same way as before but rather to change its techniques.

POLICY OF LIMITED OBJECTIVES   Today the key to planning is the recognition that the Church occupies a position of minority status. The Church realizes the inadvisability of following a policy of institutional expansion, due to the demographic increase as well as to the progressive pluralization of society. The Church has to try to slow down expansion of its own Catholic institutions and to penetrate other structures and collaborate with them as much as possible, giving to them the Christian spirit. As an example, the Catholic school system in Latin America is not trying to expand too greatly, but rather to ameliorate its own system and simultaneously to cooperate as much as possible with the state school institutions wherever such cooperation is wise.

When the Church operates its own institutions, it must spend considerable amounts of capital and use valuable personnel in administrative work, thus seeming to compete with, rather than complement, the state-operated facilities. Provided the Church can accomplish its mission without these institutions, the tactic of collaboration avoids this unnecessary outlay. Ridding ourselves of outworn institutions gives us mobility to act effectively according to the transformed circumstances of our day.

PASTORAL RENEWAL OF THE CHURCH   Besides this planning of apostolic work, we find already present in Latin America a real pastoral renewal. This is apparent in the liturgical movement, promoted for a long time through the "Collectio Rituum," which explains to the faithful in the vernacular all the liturgical ceremonies. Today it is almost commonplace in great parts of Latin America to talk about the "Misa Comunitaria," in which the faithful have more and more participation. These norms have been promoted by the bishops of Argentina, Chile, and other countries, who have published directives in order to give the faithful a more accurate and up-to-date explanation of how to participate in the Mass.

There has also been a renewal of religious feasts. Although sometimes elements creep into the celebration of these feasts that are unliturgical and more superstitious than religious, when properly conducted they represent a worthy and sincere popular expression of religion. True, in some areas these folk feasts still require some further study.

Other religious acts of worship well worth mentioning in this connection are the paraliturgical ceremonies, like those written by Bishop Cammerer. These contain directives for a weekly act of worship which may be conducted by laymen in those places where there are no priests. Ceremonies of this type have been employed in Guatemala, Argentina, Chile and other countries. This is not something completely new, since long ago laymen often worked side-by-side with the old missionaries. Carefully selected laymen were chosen to conduct certain acts of worship for the Christian community, such as baptism and instruction of the people.

A CONTINENTAL CATECHETICAL PROGRAM   Latin American countries have advanced tremendously in catechetical work in recent years. For more than three years the Latin American Institute for Catechetics has been training national and diocesan directors of catechetics. The centers of catechetics in Europe, such as Lumen Vitae in Belgium and the Catholic Institute of Paris, have been receiving many Latin Americans for their advanced training courses. The Confraternity of Christian Doctrine has been active in some countries, although its development is still at a preliminary stage. In Guatemala and in the highlands of Peru and Bolivia, and in other places, the Church has been engaging more and more laymen to do this work on a full time basis.

The more we realize that the Church in Latin America is in the state of mission in many areas, the more the Church will realize that apostolic work and the transmission of the message of God cannot be limited to the priests but must enlist the laymen to play specific and substantive roles.

For the Church to be in a state of emergency in a given area is in a way a blessing of God. Thus those in local charge are forced to re-evaluate their work and to try new methods in order to be more effective. In many places mass communications media, such as the radio, have been used to instruct and evangelize the people. Excellent results have been achieved in some of the Central American countries and in Peru, Colombia, Bolivia, Brazil and other countries.

A CONTINENTAL SPIRITUAL RENEWAL   Another achievement has been the development of the general mission in given dioceses and even in entire nations. In this work religious priests, Sisters and Brothers have collaborated with the diocesan clergy. The purpose of these missions has been not so much to bring the Christians back to the sacramental life, but, first of all, to deliver the Good News to all men, to insist that a fresh evangelization should serve as a preliminary stage to the adoption of the sacramental life by professing Christians. It has also proven a good way to search out leaders for the Christian community. Anticipating the spirit of renewal of the Ecumenical Council, many dioceses have been promoting weeks of *aggiornamento* for their priests. Many bishops have recognized that any planning of the work of the Church, especially when it presupposes a change of mind and attitude, has to be preceded by a change of attitude on the part of the priests themselves.

This renewal in the apostolic life of the Church in Latin America is also being promoted by many forms of coordination effected by the continental secretariat of the Bishops' Conference of Latin America (CELAM), with its base in Bogota, Colombia. The Latin American Conference of Major Religious Superiors likewise makes many precious contributions in various countries.

HOPE BURNS VIVIDLY   To be realistic in this vast spiritual enterprise involves a deep optimism and confidence in God. The Spirit is moving in the new Church in the new Latin America. The image this Church is giving of itself to the men of today is an image of youth, of a Church that knows that the love of God she has to give to men is not only words, but becomes incarnate in hospitals, schools, radio networks, cooperatives, institutes of social promotion, rural institutes, trade unions. The image created is that of a vibrant Church in which the freshness of the new contribution of laymen, the new engagement of all Christians in the action of the Church, assures us that the Spirit of God is still with us. In spite of all the difficulties, one great hope burns vividly: the hope that with the help of dedicated Catholics throughout the world, this work of renewal will represent the common action of all good men, a genuine symbol of unity.

CHAPTER IV

The Church Goes into the Marketplace

As recently as ten or fifteen years ago how often did we not hear the Church in Latin America described as the Church of silence? Today, instead, we find Catholic leaders consistently carrying their programs into the market place. They face up frontally to fulfilling Christ's mission in the temporal order.

Msgr. Joseph Gremillion of the Diocese of Alexandria, Louisiana, an officer of Catholic Relief Services, has for twenty years been a protagonist of the Church's socio-economic program. Since 1960 he has been intensely active in social programs in Latin America. He sets forth clearly in this chapter the Church's continental role in Latin America as regards the temporal order.

CHRIST AND THE WHOLE MAN   The same Jesus Christ Who says, "Not by bread alone does man live—," also says, "I was hungry and you gave me to eat . . ."

The same Lord and Savior who says, "See how the lillies of the field grow; they do not toil or spin; and yet I tell you that even Solomon in all his glory was not arrayed like one of these . . . ," this same Lord and Redeemer also says, "I was a stranger, and you brought me home, naked, and you clothed me, sick, and you cared for me . . ."

This same Jesus Christ lives on today, in this world in and with, by and through His Church, One, Holy, Catholic and Apostolic. The Church of Christ continues the concerns and the mission of Christ—to the whole man, body-and-soul, to all the Family of Man, here in this workaday world and through the world to come, in the orders both temporal and spiritual.

NEW ROLE FOR THE CHURCH   We shall discuss the concerns and mission of Christ in the temporal order, the present role of the Church of Latin America amidst hunger and disease, illiteracy and social disorganization, the new role of the Church as champion of the oppressed and promoter of basic economic and societal reforms, the Church as progenitor of that fundamental social justice and order which must uphold and nourish the spirit and dignity of all sons of God and all brothers of Christ, to make of us all truly one.

Indeed, this is, on the whole, *a new role* for the Church of today in Latin America; a new role in much the same way as the Church in the industrialized West began but a few decades ago to champion the rights of the wage earners over the absolutism of laissez-faire; in much the same manner as we Catholics of the United States began but a few years—even a few months—ago to champion the rights of our Negro brothers.

Here then is an experience Catholics of Latin America and of North America share—in many ways we are all fledglings in the complex duty of leadership in the temporal order. By and large we of the United States and Canada have longer experience in the reform of social and economic institutions. By and large the Catholics of Latin America have had more singular success in begetting interracial brotherhood of justice and love.

Seekers of the truth, we must rid ourselves of past notions about the Church in Latin America. She is no longer to be identified with the landed aristocracy, the political oligarchy and the oppressive status quo. In many places bishops, priests and lay leaders provide the new ferment for institutional reform. Social movements now appear which become all the more startling, and all the more hopeful, because of their sudden appearance and rapid flowering in the past five years.

CHURCH TEACHING REACHES THE PEOPLE   The authentic social teaching of the Church is now reaching the people through pastorals and public statements of the bishops acting conjointly, and through many intermediate and grass-roots teaching and training centers, often directed and manned by lay leaders, comparable to the labor schools which sprang forth in the United States and Canada during the great depression of the Thirties.

The constant theme of these teaching and formation programs is the necessity of fundamental reform of the economic, political, and social institutions—a restructuring which must be so profound, so global, so rapid and so far-reaching as to be nothing less than society-wide *revolution*, a revolution without physical violence and within democratic processes, but in truth a "folding up" of the old order and the "unfolding" of a new system of human relations, based on natural law, social ethics and Christian inspiration. In each nation the reconstruction of the social order must take into account the ethnic, ideological, economic, political and other de facto forces of that nation without doctrinaire generalization. To this end professionally staffed institutes for survey, evaluation and planning have been constituted to define goals, to determine means and to set up mechanisms for implementation. To an increasing and astonishing degree the social apostolate in Latin America is fortified by scientific and sociological research of a type not yet attained by the Church in the United States.

TWO TYPES OF APOSTOLATE These reform goals are implemented by two types of apostolate to the temporal order:

a. Direct social action programs under Church auspices like social welfare agencies, cooperatives, community development, training and adult education programs.
b. The indirect temporal apostolate of influence and action by lay leaders in the temporal order, within political, economic, managerial and technical bodies, within farm and city worker organizations, and educative agencies, to bring about constitutional, legislative and administrative reforms. In this latter case laymen act on their own responsibility in the temporal order, without formal connection with the official Church and most certainly not subject to the directives

or wishes of their spiritual leaders. And they work in concert with other citizens who share the same goals, but who do not necessarily share the same Christian ideology and motivation.

To attain their agreed civic and economic goals of savings and capital formation, of job creation and wage-profit equity, of land tenure and sharecropping reform, of technical training and leader formation, of legislative, tax and administrative advance, and to form the worker and slum unions by which the oppressed and miserable can become a potent counter-vailing force in society, these citizen leaders associate into many organizations and movements. These proliferate from national and provincial centers into the market-towns and slums, into the villages and haciendas. And the national leaders now join hands across political frontiers to beget continent-wide federations, overcoming the geographical and chauvinist isolationism of the past four centuries.

BISHOPS KNOW THEIR POOR   Christian social teaching now trumpets forth like a sudden thunder, shaking the basal struc-tures of the moribund past, already under siege by historical forces above and underground. But these pastorals of the hier-archies of Chile and Brazil, Peru and Ecuador are not merely negative blasts adding to the mounting chaos. They apply rather the optimistic building blocks of Pope John the Affirmative to the concrete realities of their respective home-lands. We see that these bishops and pastors now really know their barriadas and favelas and callampas, that they really care for the least of their flock, "les miserables" of our day.

On my arrival at the bishop's residence during a recent visit to Ecuador, a formal committee of laymen was awaiting me as a director of Catholic Relief Services-NCWC, an official agency of the bishops of the United States. These committee members were not the hacienda owners, not the wealthy merchants, nor the Knights of St. Gregory in battle array. No, the bishop had gathered around him those closest to his heart —delegates from the festering slums and mountainside farms. As can happen readily among the unlettered, ceremony was overcome, not to say crushed, and several spoke out spontaneously, "giving testimony" from the heart.

The change within the Church of their town as manifested by their own bishop was the principal theme. I saw there with my own eyes that the Church is now being recognized as Mother of the poor and Champion of the oppressed by the afflicted themselves. One lady, weary with worry, malaria and a nursing baby at her open breast, broke up the meeting. She said: "This palacio, the Bishop's Palace, is no longer reserved for the rich from the big haciendas. Now it has become *our* house, *my* house, the house of the poor." This weary mother broke up the meeting because the bishop burst into tears and left the room. And so did I.

RECOGNITION OF THE CHURCH'S LEADERS   The concurrence of present Christian social teaching and the goals of the Alliance for Progress, under whose charter all Latin American nations join hands with the United States for economic and social progress, is timely and fruitful. This is now recognized by many government leaders in Washington, among them Senator Hubert Humphrey. In July, 1963, Senator Humphrey spoke as follows on the floor of the Senate:

> Mr. President, this noon I was honored to serve as host at a luncheon for one of the great social leaders of Latin America, Raul Cardinal Silva, Archbishop of Santiago, Chile. I am happy that my colleagues on the Foreign Relations Committee and leading officials of the Alliance for Progress program were able to meet with Cardinal Silva and discuss some of the most important problems confronting the Alliance for Progress program today.
>
> Mr. President, I ask unanimous consent to have printed in the *Congressional Record* at the conclusion of my re-

marks an article from the *New York Times* describing the leadership which Cardinal Silva is providing in the movement for economic and social reform in Chile.

To give my colleagues some idea of the progressive role which the Church is now playing in many Latin American countries in promoting the aims of the Alliance for Progress, I also ask unanimous consent to have printed in the *Congressional Record* at the conclusion of my remarks a copy of the pastoral letter issued by the Chilean bishops in November 1962 advocating basic structural reforms in Chile. It is a model document for all Latin American countries to follow in implementing the aims of the Alliance for Progress. (Senate, *Congressional Record*, July 9, 1963, p. 11612 and following.)

Senator Humphrey included in the *Congressional Record* the *New York Times* report on this pastoral which begins as follows:

Dateline: Santiago, Chile.

Chile's Roman Catholic Church is trying to help solve critical political and economic problems here to improve the lot of the common man.

The move is under the leadership of 55-year-old Raul Cardinal Silva, Archbishop of Santiago, who calls for drastic social reforms.

The gist of his message is that Chile must overhaul her unbalanced social system and make great changes to ease the lot of millions of her under-privileged or the job is going to be done in totalitarian manner by Communist methods. (paragraphs 1, 2 & 3 of *Times* article.)

Despite some gains, there is general agreement here that there are gross social inequalities. But the most of the latest message from the church hierarchy is that reforms are going entirely too slowly and that too many so-called faithful Christians in Chile are showing cold indifference to problems of the masses that have now reached the emergency stage. (par. 14; "Church Demands Reforms in Chile," by Edward C. Burke, *New York Times*. International Edition, Nov. 5, 1962, p. 7.)

The bishops of Brazil issued a pastoral similar to Cardinal Silva's statement on Brazil's Labor Day, May 1, 1963, which has attracted comparable comment in North and South America. Drawing freely from *Pacem in Terris* and *Mater et Magistra*, this statement is divided into sections treating, for Brazil specifically, of rural and land reform, business and tax reform, administrative, electoral and educational reform.

THE CALL FOR SOCIAL JUSTICE The second current contribution of the Church to the temporal order of Latin America, the call for social justice, is more difficult for us North Americans to grasp for the simple reason that we of the United States and Canada have not experienced a similar historical role.

On the whole, for the past hundred and fifty years North America has enjoyed political stability and economic progress to a degree unmatched in any other part of the globe. The Church in Canada and the United States as a spiritual body has been supported and nourished by the natural life of the affluent society.

Quite the opposite has obtained in Latin America. The Church has been battered and weakened by ideological and political strife, by social and economic fossilization. In her human manifestations the Church has shared the ills of the civic body whose outmoded feudal structures have at last collapsed to produce the crisis of our generation.

The high degree of social justice which now obtains in Western Europe and North America is the slow maturing product of two centuries of struggle, marked by the highlights of the American and French Revolutions of the 1700's, the Jefferson-Jackson popular movements and anti-trust legislation of the 1800's, last century's Civil Wars, the struggles of labor and farm organizations, the New Deal of the depression years and the racial strife of our day.

In Latin America these basic advances, which required six generations in the industrialized North Atlantic Community, are being squeezed into a decade under the negative impact of today's Castro, under the positive pressure of the people's demands for justice, and under the stimulus of reform programs like the Alliance for Progress.

ABLE PROTAGONISTS OF A CONCRETE PROGRAM   The Church has set up professional centers for the survey and planning of socio-economic development, notably in Chile, Colombia, Venezuela and Northeast Brazil. This technical service, unlike anything under Catholic auspices in North America, has been inspired by persons like Fathers Lebret, Houtart and Vekemans, and is strongly supported by MISEREOR, the social development program of the German bishops, which supplies some four million dollars annually to the social action programs of Latin America.

Latin American clergy like Bishop Sales of Brazil, Father Perez of Colombia, and Msgr. Velasquez of Mexico, lay leaders like Carlos Acedo Mendoza of Venezuela, Sergio Ossa and Ramon Venegas of Chile, have in the past three years brought together highly qualified economists, sociologists, agronomists, financial, research and educational specialists. These technical teams analyze their nation and region, diocese by diocese, village and hacienda, slum by slum. Taking into account illiteracy, disease, land tenure, housing, unemployment, and revolutionary movements other than Christian, they plot out the reforms to be promoted by social action of Christian inspiration. Social action programs already functioning are strengthened; needed movements are initiated.

The various categories of national organizations like labor and farm leader formation, radio and basic education, cooperatives, agrarian reform, rural extension, housing and technical schools are able to define their own goals, and to set up the mechanisms best suited to attain these goals under the top technical consultors of these survey and planning centers.

It must be stressed that the professional centers dovetail their plans most closely with the socio-economic development programs of the national governments, regional bodies, the Alliance for Progress and Common Market initiatives. Indeed some of these centers, notably DESAL (*Centro para Desar-*

rollo Economico Social de America Latina) of Santiago, Chile, and CIS (*Centro de Investigacion Social*) of Bogota, Colombia, are now requested by governmental bodies like the Inter-American Development Bank and the Institute of Agrarian Reform to make surveys and plans for them under contract.

OUR MODEST ROLE IN THE UNITED STATES In the United States, Catholic intellectual centers have played but the slightest role in the thinking, planning and staffing of the New Deal and New Frontier, in preparing social security and the banking system, labor and farm legislation, and international programs like the Marshall Plan and Alliance for Progress. Our Catholic universities have not been creative contributors to these historic social advances, except for an associate role in the labor field. We and our nation have been the beneficiaries of Harvard, Columbia and Chicago, and other universities, foundations and institutes of social study.

While I do believe that these new Christian inspired planning centers in Latin America already show much accomplishment and greater promise, it must be stressed that these are young endeavors still subject to the judgment of the future. But for the first time in the modern era, Christian social teaching enters the temporal arena during the initial formative period of industrialization instead of attaching itself belatedly to an ongoing system, as occurred in European and North American democratic social and technical development of the past two centuries.

STRONG SOCIAL ACTION PROGRAMS A further manifestation of the Church's new role in the temporal order follows from the above: an impressive array of social action programs, promoting and implementing structural reforms, have arisen in the past decade, with strong acceleration of spread and competence in the past two years. Some of this advance is due to resources from outside, as through the Papal Volunteers of the Church in the United States and Catholic Relief Services, NCWC, in the social welfare and related fields. Great credit must go to MISEREOR and ADVENIAT, the German bishops' development programs. The German Catholics have concentrated their generous resources of more than eight million dollars on setting up national systems of technical training and leader formation, by underwriting the programs prepared by DESAL as outlined above. DESAL and its national affiliates like the Chilean Institute of Development, directed by Senor Ossa, also render valued assistance to these social action systems in obtaining donations and loans from governments, foundations, industry and labor.

Attention should be given to the radio education movement, *Accion Cultural Popular*, pioneered by Msgr. Salcedo of Colombia and now spread into ten other countries, and to the rural and labor movement in Northeast Brazil, *Servicio de Asistencia Rural*, to Father McLellan's pioneer work in credit unions in Peru, to the housing cooperatives of INVICA, Chile, to the Venezuelan Institute of Community Action, to the Mexican and other social action programs.

Importance must be given to the increasing role of Christian Democracy as expressed in the political, labor, managerial, university and civic arenas by Latin American lay movements acting within the compass of their proper authority. This role seems unusual to Catholics of the United States and often is difficult to grasp. Our own experience has been so completely different; we tend to judge them from the angle of our successful "American way of life" which has operated from another frame of reference.

Christian leaders of Latin America, clergy and lay, have in the past five years pioneered and inspired social movements of deep significance to their respective nations, to the continent, and indeed to all our hemisphere. The Church is now becoming known as the Mother of the Poor, Champion of the Oppressed, Teacher and Protagonist of Social Justice and a Human Order worthy of Sons of God and Heirs of Heaven. Despite daily headlined political instability and social near-chaos in some sectors, we have many reasons for hope and thanksgiving.

CHAPTER V

Latin America's Plea for
Vast Social Change

Seldom have we witnessed such a multiplicy of pleas for a cause by the various Catholic hierarchies of a large segment of Christendom as has come out of Latin America during recent years. We refer to the pastoral letters issued by the bishops in almost every Latin American nation on the social injustices which are very near to a common heritage of all these countries.

A layman who has played a major role in the social action program in Chile is Dr. Sergio Ossa Pretot, Director of the Chilean Institute for Development. Dr. Ossa has worked closely on socio-economic matters with Cardinal Silva of Santiago. He has been associated with the remarkable group of clergy and laity who have prepared the effective studies on Latin America's social problems that have captured a leading place for the Catholic Church in this field in Chile and throughout the continent. Dr. Ossa has supplied much of the contents of the chapter that follows.

We know the Church in Latin America today for its keen awareness of the monstrous economic unbalance under which great numbers of its members live. The Church, "mother and teacher," cannot be silent on such matters. We are proud of the Latin American bishops for this stand.

BISHOPS WITHOUT SOCIAL SENSE   But it was not always so. Bishops at the turn of the century did not hold the views of their successors of today.

It seems useful to quote some paragraphs from a document in which Dr. Casanova, Archbishop of Santiago, Chile, spoke

41

in 1891 of the "social problem," in reference to "Rerum Novarum," the encyclical of Leo XIII.

The Archbishop contended that the social problem originated in unwillingness of the poor to accept as normal and just the social differences between the classes.

"Some superficial minds," Archbishop Casanova wrote, "are easily convinced that the providential fact of the existence of social differences among men of equal nature is unjust. This false belief gives birth to a fatal antagonism between the rich and the poor, between employers and proletarians, between the fortunate and the unfortunate."

As a remedy to this dissatisfaction, His Excellency proceeds to propose the practice of certain moral virtues to be found in the Gospel. The poor, he says, should practice resignation; the rich should practice detachment from their riches. The latter must consider the poor to be their brothers and succor them in their need; the poor, in turn, should find the means for their livelihood in honest work.

Speaking of strikes and describing the evidences of socialism in Chile, Archbishop Casanova says, "For a long time now we have observed in Chile the presence of deadly germs in the form of socialist activities. More than once, unions have struck against their employers, with serious consequences to industry and to themselves in the salaries they have lost."

Thus a highly placed Church prelate of the 1890's interpreted the growing discontent then appearing among the wage earners. It is not difficult to understand how such an attitude projected an image of the Church as protector of the wealthy. It is easy to see why entire populations were gradually distanced from her.

NEW LOYALTY TO THE WORKER   However, in 1921 a favorable reaction is to be noted. Archbishop Errazuriz of Santiago, speaking of the sufferings of the proletariat and of their justified protests against injustice, expressed other sentiments.

"These evils are great evils indeed," he declared, "especially for the proletariat. The rising cost of living, the lack of resources and the frequent disregard of their need give the working people the right to press their just claims.

"The present state of affairs must come to an end, and since the victim is ordinarily unable to make his complaints heard, the Church, his natural protector, is pleased to foster the formation of associations which might enable workers to help themselves, give assistance to each other, and be defended from the cruelty of pitiless employers."

Similar reactions began to appear in other countries almost simultaneously with what came to pass in Chile, until today a vigorous fight for social justice for the entire population characterizes the program of the Church.

The worsening of living conditions in Latin America entails the direst poverty for the majority of the population, almost entirely without economic resources. Great numbers suffer a scarcity of vital energy due to malnutrition. A consequence is substantial inadequacy in intellectual and moral capacity, to which the absence of educational facilities must be added. Hence the Church raises her voice in her concern and anxiety for her children.

CALL FOR SOCIAL REVOLUTION   Because of the gravity of the situation, Churchmen throughout the continent in varying degrees favor a true revolution, not in a violent sense, but in one of rapid, profound and overall change in the basic political, juridical, social and economic structures.

Today, throughout Latin America the voice of the shepherds of the Church is clearly heard, denouncing the social ills of the hour.

"In other nations," states the Archbishop of Arequipa in his pastoral letter of May, 1963, "liberal capitalism has undoubtedly evolved, becoming more social and Christian. In Latin America, and specifically in Peru, it must be admitted that this evolution has only started. Our social legislation, for instance, has been inching its way since the beginning of the century. But it is evident that our evolution is too far behind that of other nations and is still superficial. It has not achieved a better distribution of even consumer goods, much less of production goods, that is to say, land and capital. Most especially, the serious problems of our Indian peasantry remain almost untouched."

And then, preoccupied by a retardation that may lead events along a path other than the Christian one, His Excellency adds, "The rate of present social and economic change is exceedingly slow.

"A strong political action is of the utmost urgency. This must restructure the juridical and social patterns of the country in the light of principles more in agreement with the social doctrine of the Church, and shorten the stages necessary for social and economic development of the nation."

The entire Peruvian hierarchy shares this disquiet. In its collective pastoral of the same month and year it states:

"It is urgent that a great social effort be made so that such conditions may be eliminated. If they are not solved through an effective process of improvement and development, they will prove an ever increasingly active virus that will lead to social collapse."

BRAZIL'S BISHOPS CALL FOR CHANGE A similar urgency for change is pointed out by the Brazilian bishops through the message of their National Conference of 1963; "We are faced with the need for a decisive and urgent transformation. This means the passing from one social structure to another where the human personality will recover its human dimension in the use of freedom and of the resources belonging to a dignified way of life."

Continuing they refer to specific reforms and speak of the land problem, for they deem "man's natural right to ownership to be unpostponable." They call for reform of the business enterprise, for a "growing integration of all those who share in the enterprise, its life, its property, its profits, its decisions." They recommend a tax reform, "to make income tax of a more efficiently progressive nature, adopting strong measures that will inhibit the various kinds of tax evasions or concealment."

They note the need of administrative reform because "we all feel that the Brazilian administrative machinery does not respond sufficiently to the present requirements of a country struggling in an immense effort for social and economic development." They speak for electoral reform, "decisive in the current process of purification of democratic institutions."

"These reforms," say the Brazilian bishops, "are mere stages in a global transformation towards which we must progress. They cannot be used as pretexts to confirm the existing order."

SOCIAL PASTORALS IN CHILE   This favorable reaction is also expressed in the first "social" documents of the Chilean bishops. The Chilean Church understood that her apostolate would not be integral and complete if it did not take into account the Christianization of social and economic life, the necessary basis for the dignity of the human person. Thus, in a pastoral letter of September 1932, she said: "Let us teach, propagate, announce, with all the publicity and propaganda means available, the social-economic doctrines that stem from the Gospel."

The Bishop of Talca, His Excellency Manuel Larrain Errazuriz, President of the Latin American Bishop's Council, said in a pastoral letter of 1944: "The Church, through her pontiffs, demands a deep social reform, and for an obvious reason: because present organization, in many of its aspects, is very far from being Christian. There are, in the present organization of the world, a great number of mistakes and injustices that a Roman Catholic must never accept. In the field of principles, Christian ideas on ownership and work have been forgotten and an ancient pagan concept has been substituted for them. In the field of economy, there is poor distribution of wealth, a fact that has established misery as a normal product of modern society and has created in the social field the conflict of classes, rather than the Christian concept of cooperation and harmony. In a word: social order requires a thoroughgoing reform and it is the Catholic's duty to fight for it."

In another pastoral letter written in 1946, Bishop Larrain added: "Our message must first of all state that we do not fear any just social reform that may be planned.

"Even though the Church considers tradition to be an unexpendable element of progress, she does not hold exclusively to the past, nor is she afraid of the natural evolution that is taking place."

CHILE'S NOTABLE APPEAL OF 1947   On January 1, 1947, came the notable appeal of the Chilean bishops. "The supreme goal pointed out by the social encyclicals," these prelates declared, "is the redemption of the proletariat and the reform of social life in accordance with the principles of the Gospel. To reach it, the Christian concepts of work, capital and ownership must be reestablished."

More recently we find three collective pastoral letters of the Chilean hierarchy, which again, and in very direct language, point out the urgent need for radical changes in the existing social structure.

STATEMENT ON THE RURAL WORKERS   In March, 1962, the Chilean bishops spoke on the condition of rural workers in the country.

"The problem lies," this statement explained, "in the imbalance in productive efficiency between the rural sector on the one hand and the industrial sector and services on the other, and in the distance between the way of life of the rural inhabitant and of those living in the city, so that those that till the land often feel in an inferior condition, as men depressed. It is truly regrettable that the rural worker, especially the one who works the land with his own hands, should feel displaced in the modern world. Society, in its headlong race for progress, has left him behind."

The document then pointed to the "too marked imbalance, that cannot continue without becoming a threat of violent ruptures, between the owner of the larger part of arable lands in our country and the peasant working on them. The former lives in the city almost the entire year; the latter is a foreigner in the city. Progress and comfort are for the first, not for the second."

To the Chilean bishops "conditions that the rural sector finds itself in today urgently demand thorough-going reform of the rural structure."

The two ends to be pursued are "better use of land for the community and a greater share of the peasant family in owner-ship of the land and its yield." This double purpose will im-prove man at three levels: a) the physical—better living con-ditions, healthful housing; b) the social—technical and voca-tional education, professional associations; and c) the moral —education in social meaning and responsibility in work. Consequently, land reform must reshape those structures that, because of their nature or through the evolution of the times, have become unfit to achieve such aims.

INCISIVE CHRISTIAN SOCIAL PHILOSOPHY   In July, 1962, the Chilean bishops, in another pastoral letter, noted that man is not an isolated individual but a social being, for "only in community, in dialogue with other men, can his potentialities come to prosper."

They added then: "It is in this spontaneous and consciously communitarian attitude of the true Christian that modern man, individualistic, closed in himself, shall discover true human brotherhood and the real meaning of authority."

However, their most important statement in this document on social matters touched the country's fundamental problem: "Without forgetting the urgency of other social and human needs in general, we have wished to put greater stress in one category: physical misery, resulting from the non-satisfaction of basic needs."

The pastoral letter makes special mention of employment opportunities, productive training, commensurate salaries and social compensations.

"The Christian," it reads, "to be truly so, must take a stand regarding these reforms, to be sure that social structures be such that they allow the lower income layers of the population a greater share in the fruits of the productive process. To this end, Christian man must favor the institutions for social re-vindications and, if necessary, participate in the operation of these institutions."

In the judgment of the Chilean bishops, Christians must lend their support to the necessary institutional changes, such as an authentic land reform, reform of the business enterprise, tax reform, administrative reform and similar functions.

PROGRAM OF SOCIAL REFORMS   But now let us make clear that the Church in Latin America at the present time is not content with mere preaching of the need and of the urgency of social reforms. In many cases she has sought to guide the faithful by providing a living example on how these reforms may become a reality.

In Cuzco, Peru, the Archbishop has refused offers made to him by landowners in the area to buy the Church-owned land reserved for land reform, and has declared: "The land will belong to the peasants. The plots will be given to peasants who live and work on properties of the Church as soon as it becomes scientifically possible, for it is not enough to know the social doctrine of the Church. It is also imperative that it be put into practice."

The Archbishop of Medellin, Colombia, gave all his belongings to its workers and peasants and set up quarters in a worker's neighborhood, launching a great social crusade which he named "Revolution of the Holy Cross."

During a workers' meeting, he said: "We live in a time when it is necessary to make progress at faster rates and with greater generosity, for it is a Holy Revolution against the revolution of paganism; every minute is decisive.

"There is nothing more deeply revolutionary than the Gospel. In it we find the essence of every noble transformation and of all true change so badly needed by the world."

CHURCH THE INSPIRING FORCE   In Chile it may be said that the Church has become the inspiring force of a true social democratic revolution, the only one which, while respecting the freedom of man, can oppose the advances of Marxism. Her work has also been extended to the direct or indirect promotion of operational models for reform, and the results obtained are proving their feasibility.

To attain the present position where such magnificent work of dissemination and of social promotion is being done, the Church, sometimes painfully, has had to adapt her activities and make her structure adequate to the needs of the new Chilean society moving from a predominately rural condition to an urban one (today only 30% of the population lives on the farms), and from a monolithic culture of a paternalistic nature to a new one where a number of diverging values co-exist in a pluralistic society. It is true that according to the last census taken, 85% of the population claims to be Catholic, but when these indicators are compared with true participation of the people in the Church, one finds a relative lack of penetration. Thus, for instance, an average of not more than 10% of all Chileans go to Mass every Sunday, a figure that drops to a low of 0.5% in some marginal settlements.

THE TERM "CHRISTIAN REVOLUTION"   Quite understandably, there is a difference of opinion among Latin American bishops and Catholic leaders generally regarding the use of the term "Christian revolution." It is used without hesitation in Chile while in other countries it is frowned on because it smacks too much of the Communist call for bellicose, if not violent, action.

From Cardinal Cushing of Boston we have a summary of the position of the Chilean group under the leadership of Cardinal Silva:

> Late in 1962, *Mensaje*, a Catholic magazine of thought in Chile, published a special issue entitled "Revolution in Latin America—the Christian Vision." Late in 1963 this same magazine published a similar issue of 200 pages, this time called "Revolutionary Reforms in Latin America."
> The group of talented priests and laymen responsible for these studies on present conditions throughout the

Latin American world are encouraged in their work by Chile's great Church leader, His Eminence Cardinal Raul Silva, Archbishop of Santiago. These people are driven by the strong conviction that they speak quite literally when they talk of a revolution.

"We witness," this group tells us (and there are many other able groups throughout Latin America who say the same), "an ever-growing mass of Latin Americans becoming conscious of its *misery*, conscious of the injustice of so much that in the name of the existing political, juridical, social and economic order they are obligated to accept. It is clear that this huge majority is determined *not* to accept this situation any longer. They call for a rapid and a radical change."

"And hence," this Catholic group declares, "we assert that a social revolution in Latin America is already on the march. Further, it appears to us that the most appropriate attitude for the Latin American Christian is not to close his eyes to the obvious but to confront the facts squarely and search for ways to 'Christianize' this revolution which advances with compelling inevitability."

There may be many good people in Latin America who do not accept this point of view. It frightens some, it angers others. This Santiago group is aware of this difference of outlook on the part of some and strives vigorously to explain its position.

JUSTIFICATION OF THE WORD REVOLUTION   Cardinal Cushing is at pains to quote at length the views of the Chilean group in justification of calling the Church's effort a Christian revolution:

"To Christianize this revolution already on the march," *Mensaje* explains, "means to us to free it from unjust violence, resentments, hates, egoistic selfishness. We don't stand for the suppression of freedom and the rights of man. On the contrary, we contend that this freedom and these rights should not be the monopoly of a small minority but should be extended to all Latin Americans everywhere."

If not revolution, these men ask, what other word might be used? Would it be better to talk of evolution, of restoration, of consecration to brotherly service? Such words, they answer, just won't do.

"The fact is," they assert, "that a genuine revolution is now in progress in Latin America, motivated by tremendous injustice. The people, with good reason, don't believe in *evolutions* or in vague *consecrations*. They ask for and they need a radical, integral, rapid change. Not to call it a revolution seems to us," these men declare, "to represent categoric blindness. Therefore, we talk of revolution, though of course in terms of Christian revolution."

In every field of life—the political, the economic, the educational, the social, the religious—Latin America's problems of reform are enormous. Into whatever area we look, the tasks to be done are far greater than those in similar fields of any other region in the western world.

What would I call this tremendous movement for change? I would unhesitatingly name it, as did the Santiago group of progressive priests and laity supported by their Cardinal Archbishop, "The Christian Revolution in Latin America." I pray that you shall all be identified with it. Peaceful, constructive and educational, it is the only effective answer to the Communist threat.

In Latin America's task of social reform, practically nothing escapes today from the action of the Church. The possibility for its growth and development in the future will depend on the efforts that Latin Americans make, but also, to a great extent, on the international solidarity that the more developed nations of Europe and North America will create and maintain.

CHAPTER VI

The Master Plan Arrives in Latin America

Master plans are the order of the day. The sophisticate groans in dismay when he hears that the idea has actually invaded the sacred confines of the Church in Latin America. The veteran priest or Sister who has pioneered in Latin America will undoubtedly breathe a sigh of satisfaction. He or she is aware that in view of the desperate shortages of personnel, planning can result in more effective use of the precious human elements available.

For the story of the master plan we are privileged to have the services of a master planner. This is Abbe Francois Houtart of Louvain and Bogota, director of the Belgian *Centre de Recherches Socio-Religieuses* and secretary-general of the International Federation of Catholic Institutes of Social and Socio-Religious Research. He is internationally sought after for his excellence in religious sociology. In 1952-53 Abbe Houtart studied under a U.S. government fellowship at Indiana University and the University of Chicago. Through years of assignments in Latin America he has intimate knowledge of the Church throughout the continent.

THE PASTORAL PLANS OF LATIN AMERICAN BISHOPS   In several Latin American countries pastoral plans have been prepared, elaborated and put into practice. They include the pastoral plans of Chile (1961), the emergency plan of the Brazilian episcopate (1962), the apostolic plan of the regional bishops' conference of Northeast Brazil and several diocesan plans, such as those of Natal in Brazil, Riobamba in Ecuador, San Jose de Mayo in Uruguay, Girardot in Colombia. The examples are already numerous. There are also more particular plans applying to cities, regions or even urban divisions such as south Bogota, which organized a remarkable parochial union in 1957.

WHAT IS A PASTORAL PLAN?   We all have heard of planning in the economic sphere, so necessary in areas under development. It means forecasting of the different elements that make up a material enterprise in order that they may contribute in the most adequate fashion to its successful operation. One may ask if such a study may be provided for a project concerned with pastoral care. The answer is in the affirmative though in a different manner than for an economic or social project.

A pastoral plan concerns itself with the task of evangelization or other of the aspects of parochial life. It requires in the first place an inventory of all the existing factors: number of priests, religious, church institutions, parish movements such as Catholic Action, the laity engaged in the different sectors of apostolic action, related organizations, such as schools, hospitals, social action.

Once the inventory is completed and consideration given to the social and economic factors of the region, the precise aims to be achieved must be defined.

Contrary to what many people think, the elaboration of pastoral plans can't be achieved sitting at an office desk. To fix the goals requires consideration not only of theology but of the sociological realities as well. The pastoral plans to which we have referred have all followed such a line.

It is useless to fix aims and even to determine the persons who will carry them out if those persons are not persuaded of the value of the plan and of the necessity of collaborating in its execution. This is the reason why a pastoral plan takes time to be prepared. It is necessary to associate all the elements of the base, from the parishes to the specialized Catholic Action movements. It is a real mobilization of all parties responsible for the apostolate.

Finally, a pastoral plan cannot be imposed by decree. In programs that have met with success we find that the clergy have been left completely free to accept or reject their particular role in the plan, integrated as it was in the general program. Such procedure minimizes the possibility of building up hostility through psychological causes.

WHY IS A PASTORAL PLAN NECESSARY?   The thinking of the Church on current problems, expressed in several recent pontifical declarations, has established the necessity of elaborating a general pastoral plan. More and more one speaks of a *pastorale d'ensemble*, a "pastoral master plan," an expression found in one form or another in the schemata of the Council. The problems of the evolution of the society in which we are living are now so complex that it is not possible any more to comprehend them without systematic analysis.

We have been used to apostolic individualism, the heritage of a liberal age. Each pastor has often been an absolute "boss" in his parish, each bishop in his diocese. Sectors of parallel action have been progressively established on the school level, in the workers' movements, the family movements and so forth. The coordination between the different sectors of action is not sufficient. Only through integration will it be possible to discover better adapted forms of action. It is necessary for all to be convinced that the "pastoral master plan" does not mean merely the coordination of what exists but the determination of new aims and ways of action better adapted to the present problems.

If this is necessary throughout the Church in general, how much more in a continent like Latin America? Rapid social change in Latin America requires rapid determination of key objectives for the action to be taken. The means we dispose of are so limited that it is indispensable to utilize them in the most practical way possible.

There is no question of a planification of the Holy Spirit. It is a matter of placing at the disposal of apostolic workers the various means of intelligent human collaboration, leaving their effectiveness to the will of the Lord.

WHAT SHOULD WE FIND IN THE PASTORAL PLAN? We have seen how the first pastoral plans were prepared. In Chile, a group of theologians and sociologists met during several months very regularly, totaling 30 days of work in common. They started with a summary of the socio-religious realities in Chile which had previously been prepared as part of a continental study realized in Latin America on the initiative of Msgr. Luigi Ligutti with financing from the Homeland Foundation. The theologians, confronted with these realities, elaborated in cooperation with the pastors and the sociologists a set of goals for the evangelization of Chile.

Among these goals, they recognized the need of a general mission for the whole country, to be realized over a period of about three years. This mission would present complete new methods to the nation, integrating all who were responsible for pastoral action for the purpose of provoking a renewal of the spirit as well as the introduction of these methods. A second aim was to reinforce the means for communicating the new ideas. Two agencies were enlisted: press action by the Catholic weekly, *La Voz*, and radiophonic programs, a great number of which would be distributed to the different stations. A third aim was the enlistment of public school teachers for apostolic action. These three aims were national in scope. More specific aims were also progressively elaborated for individual regions and on a local basis.

In Brazil, the Emergency Plan of the Bishops' Conference has also been elaborated with a view to the concrete situation in that country. The Brazilian plan has been less precise because the body of information available was less complete than in Chile. Since it was a much more general plan covering an enormous country, the orientation of the program was also more theoretical. Brazil was divided into seven regions with a regional Bishops' Conference for each. The various regions are elaborating their particular pastoral plans. The over-all goals foreseen in Brazil are the need of common action, the development of apostolic action by the laity and the transformation of the spirit of Catholic education. Exception must be made, however, for the Brazilian Northeast whose extraordinary achievement requires special consideration.

NORTHEAST BRAZIL, SEAT OF A PASTORAL TRIUMPH   The Northeast of Brazil includes nine states of the nation, with six hundred thousand square miles (one fifth of the national territory) and 25 million inhabitants (one third of the national population). This area possesses nine ecclesiastical provinces with 51 dioceses out of a total of 170 ecclesiastical divisions in the nation.

With the exception of the coastal area, the Northeast suffers periodically from prolonged droughts—sometimes of more than one year—provoking dramatic migrations toward other areas, e.g., toward Rio de Janeiro and Sao Paulo and toward the new capital, Brasilia.

The Northeast, more than any other area, leaves its imprint of underdevelopment on Brazil. The most eloquent indications of this underdevelopment of the Northeast are:

1. The high index of illiteracy—80 percent of the adults, and in the interior 90 percent;
2. The high index of child mortality—in Recife 232 per thousand and in the interior almost 500 per thousand;
3. The low average life expectancy of 30 years;
4. The exceptionally high birthrate, for instance in the State of Ceara, 5.3.

In order to promote socio-economic development in this area, until a few years ago systematically neglected by the Federal Government, there was recently founded the SUperintendency of the DEvelopment of the NorthEast, the famous SUDENE, which elaborated a gigantic plan—one of the most important in the world—that may, within a few years, change completely the socio-economic and consequently the moral-religious aspect of the area.

THE NORTHEAST, A POWDER KEG   At the moment, the Northeast is the most explosive area of Brazil—and perhaps of the whole western hemisphere—which Communism tries to subvert, for instance by means of the *"Ligas camponesas,"* the leftist leagues of the rural workers.

The socio-economic underdevelopment is one of the main reasons why the Church has not been able to develop normally. Thus the Northeast is also underdeveloped spiritually.

However, what nobody could have expected has happened: this poor Northeast has been the starting point of the pastoral renewal of Brazil. The important Catholic program launched here is perhaps the most successful pastoral experiment in underdeveloped areas in the world.

PASTORAL START IN 1948   This Catholic program arose from the Movement of Natal, capital of the most northeastern state, Rio Grande do Norte, which has about 700,000 souls and only 45 secular and 20 religious priests.

The Movement started when in 1948 six secular priests, under the leadership of Father Eugenio de Araujo Sales, began to meet periodically in the city of Natal in order to face together the alarming problems, particularly of the rural areas. In 1954, 33 year old Father Eugenio was consecrated Auxiliary Bishop of Natal and took over from the blind archbishop the government of the archdiocese. Thus he was able to extend his apostolic leadership to the whole secular and religious clergy of the archdiocese, bringing them together every month in a country-house on the beach for recollection, relaxation and pastoral study. First the suffragan bishops of Caico and Mossoro and then the other archbishops and bishops of the Northeast gradually found their way to Natal in order to study with Bishop Eugenio the common pastoral problems of the area. In 1962 there was officially established the Regional Pastoral Office of the bishops of the Northeast, including more than 50 ecclesiastical circumscriptions, with Bishop Eugenio the responsible Secretary.

APOSTOLIC AND SOCIO-ECONOMIC ACTIVITIES   The Natal Movement is a pastoral program with apostolic as well as socio-economic activities. Bishop Eugenio is accustomed to say: "I have long abandoned the idea that religious instruction, preaching, celebration of Mass, administration of sacraments and spiritual guidance are sufficient for evangelization. In an underdeveloped area it is indispensible for evangelization to give people general human promotion. Otherwise we will miss the mark!"

The principal apostolic activities of the Movement embrace the following: 1) religious instruction on all levels; 2) biblical and liturgical movement; 3) renewal of sacerdotal ministry; 4) strong parish life; 5) the educational system; 6) mission-preaching; and 7) campaign for vocations.

The socio-economic activities include: 1) basic primary education by means of radio-schools; 2) secondary education; 3) labor unions; 4) cooperatives; 5) handicrafts; 6) mother and child clinics; 7) agricultural clubs; 8) internal migration; 9) press; 10) radio and television.

THE TEAM OF 250 DEDICATED WORKERS   The main support of the Movement is a team of about 250 persons—part of them paid, the others volunteers—which Bishop Eugenio has built up gradually. Except for about 20 Sisters—mostly of the Good Shepherd—all are laymen of both sexes, including several university graduates and a fair number of social workers. A hundred of this team labor, scattered over a dozen social centers, in the working class districts of Natal; 39 compose the team of basic education by radio, 31 form the printing and press team, and 73 the service of rural assistance.

Bishop Eugenio himself is the leader and soul of this small but valiant army, assisted by an international team of experts, sociologists, economists, agronomists, pastoral theologians and other specialists.

Since the foundation of the Regional Pastoral Office of the Northeast, each ecclesiastical province and each diocese is building up its own pastoral office, composed of at least two priests, two sisters and two laymen. In order to promote the expansion and intensification of the Movement, the members of the Natal team fly throughout the whole Northeast, giving technical assistance to start and to perfect the apostolic and socio-economic activities of the program in the different dioceses.

JOINT PLANNING AND VISION OF THE HUMAN BEING   Among the characteristics of the Natal Movement the following may be mentioned.

1. The program is the result of *joint pastoral planning*, with participation of representatives of the whole Northeast. Every year, in January, Bishop Eugenio organizes a ten-day meeting of about 150 persons—bishops, secular and religious priests, Brothers and Sisters, and lay people of both sexes—in order to deepen the vision on the problem of the Northeast and to adapt, more and more, the existing program of action to the Northeastern "reality," mobilizing all the forces of the Church available into a "pastoral master plan." In 1963 two specialized meetings took place, one to establish the strategic points and the vital sectors of the pastoral plan of the Northeast, and another to adapt mission-preaching to the specific situation of the area.

2. The fundamental law of the Movement is the *integral vision of the human being* from all points of view, natural as well as supernatural, in perfect equilibrium, according to the hierarchy of economic, political, social and religious values. Christianity has to be incarnated in all dimensions of human life.

COMMUNITY EDUCATION AND LEADERS   3. The basic method of the Movement is *community education,* on the human as well as Christian level, because education of the individual is generally conditioned by the education of the group or family. Education of group or family, however, doesn't stand up without education of the community. This is the transposition of modern social techniques and methods to pastoral theology. All efforts are made to create real human and Christian communities and to help them to realize their own development.

Bishops, priests, Sisters and laymen frankly discussing together the pastoral problems in the diocesan spirit of a family, is one of the best expressions of this mentality.

4. Principal attention is focused on the *formation of leaders* on all levels. Bishop Eugenio built with the aid of MISEREOR a training center for leaders, where specialized courses continue without interruption, throughout the whole year, for every kind of activity of the movement. In November, 1963, a course for Sisters was given during a whole month, to introduce them to new apostolic tasks, for instance, to take over as far as possible the entire care of souls in a vacant parish. The fundamental inspiration of all these courses is the spirituality of the Movement for a Better World, which contributes in Brazil mostly to awaken the pastoral renewal of clergy and laity.

GET THE MESSAGE TO THE MASSES   5. *Poverty* leaves its specific imprint on the whole Movement, a fact in keeping with this underdeveloped area. There exists an unwritten law: "Don't invest in constructions unless it is indispensable, because it is the worst investment existing; the most efficient way to invest is to invest in formation and education!" Bishop Eugenio gave the example, when, immediately after his consecration, he stopped the construction of the new Cathedral in Natal. The example was followed by the parish-community of Sao Paulo de Potengi, the model parish of the Natal Movement, which decided, when the roof was on the new church: "Our Lord and ourselves have now a roof over us, and we are out of the rain and the sun. For the present we can't spend more money on our church. We need it for more urgent apostolic activities." Cathedral and parish-church remain unfinished to this day!

6. *Means of communication*. Press and radio play an important part in the efficiency of the Movement, particularly the radio school system. These radio schools, each with 10 to 20 pupils of 7 to 70 year olds, are run by the so called "*monitoras*," generally girls of about 16 to 17 years, who are the link between the radio speaker in Natal and the pupils. Selected with

great care among the local leaders, these *monitoras* occupy key positions in the small communities of the interior. The Archdiocese of Natal has about 1,500 of these radio schools.

INSPIRE CONFIDENCE IN THE NEEDY   Passing over in silence the results of the single activities, attention should focus on the most important result of Natal's Program as a whole.

The Movement of Natal is demonstrating to the people of the Northeast, living in sub-human conditions, that they may expect from the Church not only a better life hereafter, but also here on earth. The results of the Movement inspire the needy with confidence since the Church is, at the moment, the main factor of systematic human promotion in this area. Let us never forget that underdeveloped people follow those who give them better human conditions. If the Church gives it to them, they will follow the Christian creed; if Communism gives it to them, they will follow the red creed! Because Communism, at least in Brazil, has until this moment only agitated the masses, proclaiming human promotion, without realizing it, the Church has a splendid chance to save the Northeast for Christ and civilization.

NATAL'S CONTRIBUTION TO THE NATION   The Natal Movement has already extended its influence not only to the other ecclesiastical Provinces of the Northeast, but to the whole country. We mention only: 1) the unionizing of the rural workers; 2) basic education by radio-schools; 3) the awakening of consciousness in the rural workers, making them aware of their human dignity and human rights (with all their risks); 4) the creation of the seven Regional Pastoral Offices of the Bishops' Conference of Brazil; and last but not least, 5) the dynamic renewal of pastoral methods in general.

True, the results of the Movement have also their limits. Not everybody in the Northeast has awakened to this pastoral renewal. There are priests and bishops who continue to sleep. Not all the dioceses have organized their pastoral staff as in Natal, nor have all parishes as in Sao Paulo de Potengi. But the Movement is growing and spreading rapidly under the leadership of dynamic Bishop Eugenio of Natal, who is the point of convergence of national and international visitors, of specialists in development, of sociologists and pastoral theologians.

NATAL, A LESSON FOR THE WHOLE CHURCH   The Church in the Brazilian Northeast is awake to the tremendous human and Christian problems of the area. Its bishops form the most progressive group of bishops in Brazil, to the point that some of them, and many of their clergy as well, are labeled by reactionary elements as philocommunists!

"The Pastoral Plan of the Northeast," declares Father Tiago Cloin, C.SS.R., of Rio de Janeiro, "contains a precious lesson for the whole Catholic Church because the main pastoral task of today is not to multiply the traditional types of works: parishes, schools, hospitals, orphanages, houses for the aged and asylums. Today the Church needs a creative pastoral activity which follows new ways courageously and aims at the rapid transformation of society.

"This will only be possible by renewed theological reflection on the contents of revelation on the one hand, and by continuous analysis of the socio-religious 'reality' on the other, because these are the two poles of all authentic pastoral theology, which by definition is: the incarnation of the divine message in a concrete existing human community."

GENERAL RESULTS FROM PASTORAL PLANS   The pastoral plans are still very young, but already remarkable results can be noted. It is certain that in Latin America one has been able to go much further than in the majority of the other regions of the Church. Perhaps the urgency of the needs has resulted in a clearer comprehension of the problems. In Chile, for example, the three major goals set have been realized to an extraordinary degree. The general mission throughout the nation has now been almost finished and the participation of the lay people and the religious in this work has been very great. The improvement of outlook on the pastoral program has reached beyond all expectations. The Catholic weekly, *La Voz*, now occupies one of the most important positions among the journals of Chile; technically it is one of the best. The radio programs are operating in full career and the apostolate among the teachers of the state schools is well advanced. In view of the demographic explosion, reaching the children through government school classrooms is often regarded as more important than the multiplication of Catholic schools.

In Brazil the results of the bishops' emergency plan are also very encouraging. The regional Conferences have been established and several have elaborated very specific pastoral programs. Results in the different specialized sectors have also been achieved. The progressive clarification of policy toward Catholic education is registering advances. Integrated programs in Northeast Brazil and in the Ecuadorean Diocese of Riobamba well illustrate the value of planning in getting maximum results from pitifully limited resources.

TWO CONCLUDING OBSERVATIONS   To further this pastoral planning, two concluding observations need to be made:

1. The Catholic peoples of Europe and North America who seek to help the Latin American episcopate to serve their flocks should reveal special interest in aiding the Latins to prepare diocesan, regional and national plans. An effective form of cooperation from outside consists in furnishing technicians and funds to aid in pastoral planning, especially on the theological and sociological levels.

2. Religious congregations of men and women and bishops of Europe and North America should encourage Latin American Church leaders to provide them with at least simple outlines of their diocesan plans. Armed with such, those who have precious personnel to contribute to the strengthening of the Church in Latin America will make wise decisions in placing them. Every superior who disposes of a priest, Brother, Sister or layman desires to send such personnel to areas where careful plans have been made for their apostolate.

CHAPTER VII

Catholic Schools and a Study on Basic Education

At the CICOP sessions it was very evident that there was great interest in the Catholic schools of Latin America. In this chapter essential information on education at the continental level is provided from the study of Dr. Gabriel Betancur, the distinguished Colombian authority now an officer at the Paris headquarters of UNESCO. Catholic education data is cited as compiled by the Inter-American Confederation of Catholic Education (CIEC).

One of the most effective speakers at Chicago was Miss Marina Bandeira, a pioneer in basic education in Brazil. She presented in masterful fashion the story of the extraordinary development by MEB in Brazil of the radio educational techniques worked out originally by Msgr. Salcedo in the mountains of Colombia. This study completes the chapter.

DO CATHOLIC SCHOOLS MAKE LEADERS? "I am not a school man," remarked one of the participants at the CICOP Conference. "I have been in the social apostolate eleven years. But I continually hear at this type of gathering the thrust against education in the formal sense of the word.

"People speak here of 'building the Church rather than schools or even churches.' Every one of us is the product of an educational institution. I've directed hundreds of young people who've dedicated their lives to Christ, and the great majority came from the institutions we tend to condemn.

"An undertone in the Conference here says, 'Let's get down with the people. Let's be Christ among the people. In Latin America, quite as here in the United States, these old institutions where we keep all these priests and nuns as teachers in what is known as the Catholic school system—that's a waste of time.'

"It seems to me that we are cutting off our own noses when we voice such utterances as, 'Let's get out and save the world in the market place. You teachers in your ivory towers are spoiling your substance.' "

"I don't think, Father," a fellow participant replied, "that there's any attempt to abolish the Catholic educational system. There's merely a stronger complaint in these days that our Catholic school system today does not produce the right kind of leadership. It could, but it doesn't. There is a desire to re-examine the Catholic educational system as it serves both the United States and Latin America."

"In Argentina where I hail from," said Father Luis Dolan of the Passionists in Buenos Aires, "I can't say that the leaders of our Catholic movements have always come out of our Catholic schools. I think we share your experience. We are not being taught what the presence of Jesus in 1964 should mean in our lives. We must put leadership into our schools, into our churches. But how do we bring this about? How does Jesus become a living reality? How do we inspire those thousands of boys and girls from so many loyal Catholic families? I'm only a missionary, not an educator, but I think this is our crucial problem."

"ONLY THE RICH HAVE PRIVATE SCHOOLS"   "I direct a question to Dr. Calvani of Venezuela," ventured a discussant. "In view, Doctor, of the fact that one of the problems in Latin America is the concentration of the wealth in the hands of the few and, further, of the urgent need of a well-formed Christian laity, why do you suppose a community of Sisters in Brazil recently closed a school engaged in teaching the aristocracy? Since some at least among the wealthy would seem to be the people who might aid in the proper distribution of the national resources and in the prosecution of the much-needed social revolution, it seems particularly important to make as many as possible among the wealthy into well-formed Christian leaders."

"What you say proves the necessity of a general plan," Dr. Calvani replied. "Without knowing the plan of the area involved, one could not judge the wisdom of the move made by the Sisters. But if sufficient provision already exists for teaching in a given community, or if still graver needs of another variety have arisen, the Sisters would certainly seem justified in closing their school.

"Usually our private schools in Latin America receive no support from the State. The Catholics themselves must pay for Catholic school instruction. Hence with the map of any city one may discern the pattern of Catholic education. The sections where the poor live have few Catholic grade schools and no colleges while the neighborhoods of the wealthy are well dotted with schools. Thus the Communists gain credence for their charge that the religious communities serve only the rich and powerful.

"The planning for better balance needs to begin with the parish lines. Often the priest in the parish that serves only the poor has no money even to eat, let alone conduct a free or low-fee school. The parish of the rich possesses education in abundance. Even when a primary school is provided for the poor, the low-fee secondary school, so important during those years when it is dangerous for the young man to attend public school, is not available.

"I strongly recommend seeking to form loyal Catholic teachers for the secondary schools of the public educational system. The anti-clericals and the Marxists make great efforts everywhere to win the secondary school teachers. In Venezuela we have had success in penetrating this field."

RELIGIOUS INSTRUCTION IN STATE SCHOOLS   "How is it," asked Father Rahm of El Paso, Texas, "that in these countries where it is possible for Catholics to do so, we fail to put good religious instruction into what we know in the United States as the public school system?"

"This is a good question," commented Father William Ferree of the Marianists, former president of the Catholic University of Ponce, Puerto Rico. "Often today this may be successfully achieved.

"But we frequently fail to take note in the United States of the fact that during a great period of the past and in certain areas even today, it is the tendency in Latin America for opinion on religion to polarize. Until the recent birth of the movement of Catholic renewal, everything that was not officially Catholic was anti-Catholic. In this tendency to polarize lies largely an answer to your question. If a person wanted to do something of a social nature and was not interested in doing it in a Catholic way, he would normally join not only a non-Catholic but an anti-Catholic group to do it. So it is that while religious instruction in public schools has long been permitted by law, it has been regarded in many areas as difficult if not impossible to arrange. Thank God, this specific Latin American phenomenon is changing as the Church assumes a role of initiative rather than of mere defense."

COMMENTS ON THE CATHOLIC UNIVERSITY   Quite apart from opinions pro and con on Catholic education, it exists as a fact of life in Latin America. With dispassionate recognition of this, Msgr. Ivan Illich, founder and director of the Center for Intercultural Formation at Cuernavaca, Mexico, appraises one facet of the Church's educational system, the Catholic university.

"We have to distinguish two functions in Latin America's Catholic universities," notes the Monsignor. "First they represent an institution which people frequent to follow classes. They are also an institution whereby the Church becomes intellectually present within the nation's society of thinkers. . . . These two functions are to be considered as quite separate from each other. We cannot overlook the fact that the Church's role of pastoral action includes the university world.

"Until the period of independence, the Church in Latin America held a monopoly on university training. Post-independence governments took away that monopoly and today the Catholic university in a number of countries serves in turn to break the government's educational monopoly.

"What we in the United States call student unions have in Latin America a totally and incomparably different function than in the United States. . . . The state universities are highly vulnerable to student control. Politics play a big role and absorb a lot of the students' time.

"In Catholic universities student unions are not allowed, or at least are kept under strict control. Therefore, high academic standards can be attained and more continuous teaching can be achieved on the part of the faculty.

"The disadvantages should likewise be listed. Generally the Catholic university creates the image that it is meant for those who can pay a little more, those who want special education for their children, those who want their children to learn how to make a career and a social place for themselves. Such universities tend basically to serve the upper class and to be less concerned about the social revolution concerning which there is currently so much talk.

"A second disadvantage stems from the fact that Catholic universities are finding out how tremendously expensive modern education has become. Thus they sometimes have to be satisfied with second-rate education.

"Thirdly, the mere presence of a Catholic university in a so-called Catholic country at times introduces the idea of a divisory factor in the educational field. . . . However unintended this impression may be, the impression can cause very serious damage to Catholic universities all over Latin America."

MEASURING LATIN AMERICAN EDUCATION   Whatever may be our particular angle of interest regarding Latin American education or regarding the role of Catholic education in Latin America, all of us seek fundamental data that make it possible for us to measure the dimensions of the educational task.

These dimensions are colossal. Illiteracy, for instance, is estimated by the specialists as embracing fifty to seventy million Latin Americans 15 years or older. The continental average is 43%, more than two out of every five. Dr. Gabriel Betancur, the distinguished Colombian educational authority, is now dealing with the broad lines of Latin America's education at the Paris office of UNESCO. How, asks the Doctor, in the face of such appalling prevalence of illiteracy can many of the countries of Latin America proceed to solve their other key problems? In setting up the political and social structure of a modern state, or the technical structure for modern industry and commerce this heavy percentage of people who cannot read or write represents an enormous handicap.

SCHOOL ATTENDANCE IN LATIN AMERICA   The school age population, that part which was at school in 1960, ran as follows:

Age level in years	School-age population	School enrollment	% of enrollment
5-14 years	33,247,000	26,089,000	78%
15-19 years	25,133,000	3,698,000	15%
20-24 years	17,073,000	521,000	3.1%
Totals	75,453,000	30,308,000	40.16%

Thus it is indicated that as of 1960, 78 out of every 100 children five to fourteen years of age were in primary school. But only 15 out of every 100 young people aged 15 to 19 were in middle school. And only 3 out of every 100 aged 20 to 24 were in the university. The emphasis throughout Latin America is on the improvement of middle school attendance; without this there is no hope of a consequent heavy increase in trained public leaders.

In 15 Latin American countries the grade school child averages only two and a fifth years in the classroom before dropping out; only 20 out of every 100 finish grade school. Principal reason for dropping out is to go to work on the family farm or to find some sort of a job if the family lives in the city.

A COMPARISON WITH THE UNITED STATES   Dr. Betancur notes that while only 15% of the boys and girls of middle school years enter middle school in Latin America, 90% attend junior high or high school in the United States. Of those who start in Latin America, only 22 out of every 100 finish the course. Dr. Betancur observes that in the United States 35% of the men and women of university age (20 to 24 years) are at school as against the three per cent of this age division following courses in Latin America.

Dr. Betancur in his recent study* analyzes the weaknesses in the educational system in the nations of Latin America. A major difficulty, he explains, is lack of enough teachers and the large percentage of poorly trained teachers among those available. True, in the grade schools of Argentina, Uruguay, Chile, Panama and Costa Rica at least 80% of the teachers carry certificates. In the other nations at least six out of every ten of the grade school teachers possess no teaching certificates. In the middle schools seven out of every ten professors are without a certificate or do not possess specific pedagogical training in the course they teach. At university level the situation, with honorable exceptions, is still worse. Many of the professors occupy chairs as a marginal occupation, often with the disastrous consequences which this system entails. Lack of funds for salaries is the principal explanation.

LATIN AMERICA'S OUTLAY FOR EDUCATION   Dr. Betancur makes an estimate of the present gross financial outlay for all education in Latin America both governmental and private. He includes in his figures all the Catholic schools, which teach some five million students or somewhat less than a sixth of the students at school in Latin America. His total outlay comes to

---

* A resume of Dr. Betancur's analysis appears in *Mensaje*, October, 1963, p. 572.

$1,646,000,000 a year, approximately one and two thirds billions.

This figure represents a per capita expenditure of barely more than $50 a year per person in training, from the grade school child to the university. And it provides not a penny for the tens of millions not yet in school. Thus he eloquently dramatizes the gross inadequacy of the financing of this department of Latin American life. Dr. Betancur speaks for all Latin American leaders when he points up the significance of education. "Education," he says, "is the soundest cure for poverty, discontent and every form of violent social revolution. It demands many more thousands of millions of dollars but education is the investment that pays the biggest economic and social dividends. A country's greatest wealth is the talent of its citizens. A country's most costly error is failure to educate its sons and daughters adequately."

THE CATHOLIC ROLE IN LATIN AMERICAN EDUCATION   Catholic education today occupies a relatively large place in the total educational effort of the Latin American world. According to the Inter-American Confederation of Catholic Education (CIEC), Catholic universities provide 15% to 20% of Latin American university education. From 40% to 65% of the middle school education in the various countries is provided by Catholic institutions at this level. From 10% to 20% of primary education is Catholic.

True, the Catholic contribution varies from country to country and represents a widely diverse impact on the educational life, exactly to what degree it is not clear. The lack of pertinent data is noted in a CIEC report:

> We possess no serious over-all study that establishes the educative force of the Church at this moment. This grave deficiency was visibly evident at the UNESCO conference in Santiago in 1963 when it was impossible to present a continental panorama of Catholic teaching activities. Neither was it possible to provide a concrete perspective of the role Catholic teaching will play amid

the social changes of the day. One could not judge the relation of Catholic education to the modern initiatives, plans and programs in basic education that many Latin American nations are currently promoting.

There is a lamentable division among us, a dispersal of our forces. Coordination is lacking particularly between national secretariats of the episcopacy and the colleges conducted by religious communities.

There are, as well, deficiencies of a technical and pedagogical order, as regards the quality of teaching programs and the competence of faculty members.

A marked exclusivism is noticeable, particularly in middle school institutions. Often these are devoted only to the upper classes, usually at very high cost. This leads to a reproach of the Church that its educational system appears to serve as an instrument for the prolongation of a social situation now unacceptable, given the strong current throughout the continent for a democratization of education.

EDUCATIONAL GOALS FOR CATHOLICS   With this sobering appraisal of the present position of Catholic education in Latin America, CIEC presents a set of educational goals:

1) Assure the practical and effective union of national and international organizations currently at work in the field of Catholic education;

2) Launch as quickly as possible a Latin American statistical survey of Catholic teaching activities;

3) Elaborate an over-all plan for the development of Catholic education in Latin America conformable with current social changes and with the rapidly growing socio-economic development on the continent;

4) Insure, through lay representatives possessed of capacity and effective influence, the presence of the Church in official circles, national and international, which occupy themselves with the orientation of educational goals in the individual countries and throughout the continent;

5) Achieve the integration within the educational plans of the Church of the national and continental pro-

grams for basic education, adult education and the elimination of illiteracy;

6) Permanent representation of the Church in the continential bodies of the United Nations and the Organization of American States charged to guide and promote these initiatives herein proposed;

7) Make the living presence and educative action of the Church operative and dynamic before the eyes particularly of the Christian elements in the governments of our American nations and those of Europe;

8) Integrate Catholic teaching activities into the national pastoral plans and programs of the Church throughout the continent.

A DISTINCTIVE CONTRIBUTION IN BASIC EDUCATION   This frank declaration of inadequacy and delineation of bold new goals is becoming ever more characteristic not only of educational circles but of every department of the Church's life in Latin America. The result is an imaginative approach to problems that is creating distinctive institutions of achievement in Latin America not found in exactly the same form in any other part of the world Church.

This fact is illustrated by developments touching goal number five among the above eight outlined by CIEC, namely, in national and continental programs for basic education, adult education and the elimination of illiteracy. Catholic agencies have made a unique contribution by the establishment of networks of radio schools for the teaching of the poor of the cities, the peasants of the rural districts and the mountaineers lost in the labyrinthine confines of the Andes.

Today in sixteen out of the twenty nations of Latin America Church people operate some form of radio teaching. Over forty different networks serve more than 10,000 radio "schools" that are engaged in conveying elementary instruction to many thousands of persons young and old.

THE MIRACLE OF SUTATENZA   The original such enterprise and by far the largest today is Radio Sutatenza, operated by an organization called Cultural Popular Action. It was founded in

1947 by Msgr. Jose Joaquin Salcedo in the little mountain village of Sutatenza eighty miles from Bogota, the capital of Colombia. Msgr. Salcedo's parish totaled 8,000 souls, scattered in tiny hamlets throughout the high Andes. It was physically impossible to assemble these people for school or worship or any other purpose. Monsignor passed the word that he was going to speak to them and teach them by radio.

At first in very crude fashion and later with consummate skill he was reaching tens of thousands throughout the mountains. His achievement had something of magic about it; it caught the imagination of the entire Colombian nation. Today it is a $3,000,000 enterprise with aid from the Church, the government and private foundations.

Soon the idea passed to other lands, sometimes in modest form, sometimes with a skill that proved much more meaningful than the mere elimination of illiteracy. Probably nowhere has it assumed more fascinating proportions than in Brazil under the title of the *Movimento de Educacao de Base* (MEB).

BRAZIL, SETTING FOR THE DEVELOPMENT OF MEB   For the story of MEB, we are fortunate to have an able study on this extraordinary project by Miss Marina Bandeira, who has labored on its Rio staff from its humble beginnings. This is her description of the situation:

> Brazil is an underdeveloped country with areas of extremely fast development. In the south of Brazil, especially Sao Paulo and Guanabara (Rio de Janeiro) there is a rapid industrial growth. Brazil is self-sufficient in the production of cars and trucks. The production of steel is increasing rapidly. Large power plants have been built and new ones are under way.
>
> The growth of Brazil's gross national product is indicated by the rates reached during the last few years: 6.9 in 1957; 6.6 in 1958; 7.3 in 1959; 6.3 in 1960; 7.7 in 1961. In 1962 it went down to 3.4.
>
> In recent years new roads have been built connecting the coast with the interior. One of them cuts across the Amazon forest and it now possesses regular bus lines operating there. National airlines cover the country. The

new capital, Brasilia, allowed the awakening of an immense and rich area that was isolated from the rest of the country when the only existing contacts were by ox-cart or light planes.

DISINTEGRATION OF THE EXISTING SYSTEM   The rapid changes that are taking place in some areas have allowed the improvement of the standard of living of some urban workers. The influence of radio and the contacts made possible by the new roads tend to accelerate the disintegration of the existing system: the traditional dual society where the minority holds power and the majority is kept down, outside the political and economic life of the country.

Close to the "aristocratic class," a small middle class has appeared but, as a rule, without the possibility of reaching the higher levels of influence to which they aspire. This middle class is found mainly in the large cities where we also find a high percentage of the marginal population.

The demographic explosion we are witnessing accentuates the unfortunate mal-distribution of wealth and the faults of this society where the rich are getting richer and the poor becoming poorer.

SICK ECONOMY   We cannot forget the problems created by the excesses of capital—national and foreign—in a country that does not have proper anti-trust laws. The problem of the deterioration of the price of Brazilian exports does not help. Another key to understanding the situation has been the incapacity of the ruling sector over a long period of time to carry through an overall plan for the development of the country.

If we were allowed a comparison, we might recall that the United States during the last century underwent great development, fostered by the industrial revolution, and even had to go through a civil war because of resulting social and economic problems. But the United States carried out these changes without having to suffer the exertion of any great external influence. Today the international tensions are reflected in the election of any labor union in the remotest sugar-cane plantation in the interior of Brazil. Some elements may be tools of Communist agitators, and others may handle money and peddle ideas handed out from those who retain power, abusive power, and proclaim the benefits of free enterprise and preach democracy.

SOME CHARACTERISTICS OF THIS HOUR   The following aspects are singled out as characteristic of this hour deeply marked by change:

a) The existence of areas where agriculture is carried out with ancient methods and where society obeys age-old patterns. In a few of these areas new industries are rising, new influences are being felt, and people are giving evident signs of dissatisfaction—after knowing the existence of other, better, standards of living. The people are abandoning the fatalistic attitude and demanding their share of the riches.

b) They are becoming aware of their rights: the Peasant Leagues, the urban and rural unions, the preaching in favor of land reform, are breaking down the old style relationship between employers and employees in the discussions to settle new wages and new work contracts and the like.

c) These manifestations are clear, and in some areas have become acute. They will become contagious wherever there is a man who begins to worry about the sad lot of his fellow men. This man will *fight* for justice.

BRAZIL'S BASIC EDUCATIONAL MOVEMENT   With the foregoing background on current conditions in Brazil, Miss Bandeira now moves to a description of MEB, Brazil's basic education movement:

To understand the work of the Basic Education Movement (MEB) we must bear in mind the picture above outlined.

MEB was not born to be another tradition-loaded movement, to sustain what exists at any price. It stands for the necessary changes. It stands for the full participation of the peasant and urban workers in all the matters that concern them.

MEB is not just another campaign against illiteracy. It fights against illiteracy to help destroy this chance event. But MEB dedicates its best efforts to something much deeper. Basic Education, as MEB understands it, aims at helping a human being to open his own eyes, to look for and understand his own problems, using his own initiative, walking with his own feet, with consciousness. It is a special type of adult education that reaches men that have the need, not only to read and write and to become acquainted with some techniques that are essential for their work: MEB also has the mission of helping men to interpret the social situation that is conditioning their life and their destiny.

To explain better what we mean, one must speak of the inculcation of conscientious responsibility—that is, the discovery that makes a man aware of his value as a human being, of his problems, his duties, his rights, including the right to fight for a just solution for his problems. To assume responsibility firmly is a clear sign of "conscientization."

Having found his own value, human and eternal, a man will find not only a style of life, a basic behavior, but the need to assert himself. Man discovers that apathy is harmful and isolation is a deadly selfishness. MEB, therefore, is also fundamental education for social organization. Step by step, MEB educates people to resolve the basic problems of health and work, of their relationships in the family, on the land, and in the presence of God.

THE ORIGINS OF MEB   In the year 1958, the National Secretariat for Social Action of the National Conference of Bishops of Brazil promoted the first meeting of Catholic radio stations. The National Association of Catholic Radio Stations (RENEC) was founded. This new organization which represents today more than 80 radio stations, set up a department responsible for giving assistance and support to efforts connected with radio schools which were beginning in Brazil, based on the Colombian experience of Sutatenza.

After a period of experimentation and testing and collecting relevant data, this service felt it was in a position to extend its activities. In 1961 a project and budget were accepted by the President of the Republic and acknowledged by a Decree and various agreements signed by MEB with the Ministries of Education, Health, Agriculture and other organizations.

MEB was born as a service of the Bishops' Conference but has today its own legal status, linked very closely with the Bishops' Conference. Its Board of Directors is constituted of bishops. The work itself, however, including the administrative, financial and technical aspects is the reponsibility of lay people.

THE ORGANIZATION OF MEB   Miss Bandeira's report continues:

> Throughout the whole organization, including administration, MEB does its utmost to obtain the greatest possible decentralization. The whole organization is carried out in such a way that responsibilities are distributed and decisions are made at national, state, and local levels.
>
> The object of this system is, not only to obtain the best possible adaptation of the work to the characteristics of each different area, but mainly to give the different teams the possibility to show their capacity and test the possibilities of promoting the most able people within MEB.
>
> A radio-school system (i.e., a group of schools receiving the broadcasts from one central sending station) supposes:
>
>   a) A preliminary, indispensable work consisting of:
>   —The study of local problems
>   —Meetings with the local leaders and authorities
>   —A well-adapted publicity
>   —The choice of personnel
>   b) The organization of a supervisory team with the following responsibilities:
>   —Close study of the area

—Preparation and transmission of the radio programs

—Organization and execution of the administrative work

—Selection and training of monitors and maintenance of constant contact with them

—Supervision of the radio schools

—Preparation of reports and study of the results for the National Center

c) A group of well-trained monitors:

The monitor must be a person from the local community who is willing to render service free. He is the pivot of the group of pupils that follow the radio transmissions because he is the link between the teacher and the pupils. The monitor must be intelligent and capable, and, even if most of the time he can barely read and write, he must have leadership qualities and have a sense of responsibility. The monitor enrolls the pupils, marks their presence each day, follows carefully the instructions given by the teacher: writes on the blackboard, sends pupils to the blackboard, corrects the exercises.

d) The radio school exists in very rudimentary conditions:

—A social center room, a parish hall, a private house or any other shelter available

—A transistor receiver which allows the organization of schools where there is no electricity

—Material such as elementary textbooks, a blackboard, copybooks, chalk and kerosene lamps.

CONTENT OF PROGRAMS   There are, as a minimum, two periods of four months each during which are given the rudiments of Basic Education. After the second cycle the pupil should be able to read short texts, write a small composition using his own words and be able to add, subtract, multiply and divide, besides having awakened to his role of man within the society. Each daily lesson lasts about an hour for each different class, as there are systems that have reached other grades. For the basic eight month period the subjects provided are the following:

   a) Teaching to read and write, elementary arithmetic
      —Health and nourishment
      —Living habits (house, family, community)
      —Relations with his fellowmen (types of association: unions, clubs)
      —Work (professional information)
      —Spiritual development
   b) "Conscientization" of the people, leading the pupils to:
      —Discover the value of men as sons of God
      —Awaken to their own problems
      —Look for solutions themselves
      —Assume their responsibility in the raising of the standard of living of their community
   c) Stimulate the organization of groups destined to represent the community: unions, cooperatives, mothers' clubs, etc.

PERSONNEL   Brazil cannot as yet count on a large number of highly specialized experts. MEB has to look for people with initiative and imagination, with some type of previous studies and a great capacity for dedication. Time cannot be lost on new courses that would take many years. MEB has to depend on "semi-specialized experts" and, whenever possible, give opportunity for further studies for those who have proved capable and can be spared at a given time. The majority of the people who work with MEB come from the Catholic Action Movements.

The selection of new people is made by the National Team which includes teachers, anthropologists, sociologists, psychologists, philosophers, economists, experts in audio-visual techniques, etc. The members of this team travel constantly, to organize new state and local level teams and supervise the work. When a new state or local team is organized, the new group must go through an intensive training session prepared by the national team.

The number of people who constitute the national, state and local level teams is	471
The total number of radio stations operating with MEB is	25
The total number of systems	53
Number of radio-schools	7,353
Present number of pupils	180,000
Average cost for each pupil	US $10.00

The constant evaluations of the work have shown the Brazilian sponsors of MEB that the principles followed and techniques applied are valid. But the greatest encouragement comes from the direct results of the work which, through the efforts of the state and local teams and monitors, reaches the pupils and sees them marching forward. Eloquent are the words of a typical peasant pupil who cried, "I could not sleep last night because I had discovered that I was a man!" Many pupils have become monitors, others have become leaders of local unions, all have gained in their humanity.

In these days of difficulty, which easily breed demagogues from the extreme right and the extreme left, people are learning that they must depend on their own good judgment and strive for justice.

The true meaning of the word love must regain its proper place in history. The law of "a tooth for a tooth, an eye for an eye" must at last give way to the law of "love thy neighbor and be just as unto thyself." This language of justice brings out contradictions in the face of current teachings. It means dislodging and altering structures, it means renewal of ways of thinking and ways of action.

In our work we feel the need for a new spirituality, a spirituality that could be called the spirituality of underdevelopment, which should come as the result of the study of technology in connection with the sociological facts of our underdeveloped countries, which refuse to remain underdeveloped any longer.

MEB is quite aware of the fact that it must live in a state of constant revision, correcting faults, discovering new techniques to be applied in entirely new fields that demand permanent efforts, constant study and capacity to adapt. But we feel that we are doing much more than just teaching how to read and write, because MEB is contributing to show the value of the human being, the dignity of the sons of God, the right to equal opportunity for the human life we defend.

‘

CHAPTER VIII

Confrontation of Families
North and South

One of the outstanding institutions of the Catholic Church in the United States is the Christian Family Movement. So likewise in Latin America the Christian Family Movement represents a very popular development. It is currently organized in 18 Latin American countries and is particularly strong in Argentina, Brazil and Mexico.

The national directors in Mexico are Senor and Senora Jose Alvarez Icaza whose charm and humor at the CICOP conference won them many friends. With the assistance of confreres in Mexico they have prepared comparative social data on family life in both Latin America and the United States. Thus they make it possible for us to establish a confrontation of living conditions in these two worlds which, despite their proximity, are economically widely apart. This confrontation constitutes the scope of this chapter.

"THE OPEN FAMILY" Senora Alvarez Icaza tells this revealing story:

> Just a few months ago, a thief entered our home. He managed the outside door quite easily since it had been left open by the children in the excitement of saying good-bye to my husband and myself as we left for a morning meeting of the Christian Family Movement.
>
> After entering the house, which has the good fortune of being visited constantly by our lay friends and priest friends from all over the world, the thief suddenly ran into several of our children who were playing in the hall-way. The children looked up at him and smiled brightly

as though it were the most natural thing in the world to find him there. They began to climb all over him and to ply him engagingly with questions.

"Who are you? Where did you come from? Why have you come to our house? How come you entered without calling us?" Evidently after a first brief moment of terror our thief, through the loving warmth of our children, won back his confidence. After the initial disconcerting surprise he slipped into the happy spirit of the children and glibly manufactured a tale to fit the occasion.

"Your papa is my godfather," he explained, "and I have come to get a typewriter that he told me to fix."

"You are out of your mind," exclaimed the children. "All our typewriters are in the office. Didn't anybody tell you? But come with us if you'd like; we can show you other machinery that you can fix."

And thus they went from room to room, pushing Mr. Thief through the whole house. They showed him everything, all the appliances, their toys, their beds, the paintings and religious statues that we love so much, just everything. They were enchanted with their visitor. They did not notice at all how anxious, nervous and uneasy he was. At one point in the house, the party ran into some servants who were busy about their household tasks. The stranger seemed such a great friend of the children and so much at home that the servants naturally took him for a relative or friend of the family.

All hope gone of booty of any sort, our thief finally decided to escape as quietly as possible from this home that gave him such a reception. But when he tried to leave, the children wouldn't let him go, climbing all over him. One tot picked up a toy pistol and shot him. "Boom! Boom! You can't go now," the child cried. "Fall down because I just shot you." Throwing all pretense to the winds the thief ran from the house.

When we returned home, the children all talking at once told us of the friendly visit of our godson! We soon realized that we were involved in the terrible case of the frustrated thief.

"How could this lone man go all through our house?" we asked the cook.

"Well, ma'am, we thought he was some friend of the children who had dropped in for a visit. After all, there are so many different people who come here and the children call them all uncle."

MORAL OF THE WELL-TREATED THIEF   Senora Alvarez Icaza then proceeded to draw the moral of her story for the participants at the CICOP conference:

How explain this attitude of our children, of the cook, of everyone else in our house? The answer is very simple. For the last four years, we have been involved in the Christian Family Movement throughout Mexico. One feature of the Movement is the development of the so-called "open family." By this we mean the opening of our home to our friends and to many more whom we make our friends and the introduction of our family circle to an awareness of all the rumblings of the community outside our home that make up the social order of our day.

We are now beginning to reap some of the good harvest of this philosophy of the "open family." We know that everywhere in Latin America there is a similar movement in this direction.

It is just a little over five years since the Christian Family Movement began to march in Mexico. In this five years it has enlisted almost 10,000 families. We are beginning everywhere in Latin America to experience a change, to witness many tiny evidences of a Christian renewal of family life, a rebirth of vigorous Christian living. Our Christian Family Movement already reaches into the various levels of Latin American society.

Leaders of the Christian Family Movement hold that the most profound transformation is achieved when the family determines to transform itself in truly Christian fashion and through the family influences the various elements of society for an eventual transformation of all social life.

We need food, housing, clothing, education, economic aid, many things, but we shall not profit from any of these things unless our family life is strong. This is the basic tenet of our Christian Family Movement.

A CONTINENT OF HIGH-QUALITY FAMILIES   A leading educator in Sao Paulo, Brazil, Father Corbeil of the Canadian Holy Cross Fathers, is wont to testify to the high quality of family life within segments of the population in Brazil.

"There is a certain Catholic elite in Brazil," explains Father Corbeil, "which I regard as superior in culture, religious and otherwise, to anything I have encountered in the United States and Canada, excellent though our Catholic life in North America may be. It ranks with the best in the Catholic world. I greatly admire this minority that insists always on the optimum in quality."

This statement is quoted because zealous Catholics in Latin America, more perhaps than anywhere else in the world, tend to be the innocent victims of the statisticians. As an instance, let us say that twenty million Catholics in Latin America go to church on Sunday. Immediately many a statistician will subtract this figure from Latin America's mass Catholic population of 200 million and announce to the world that here is a continent where 180 million Catholics don't go to church. The world thus rushes to its well-advertized conclusion—that in Latin America practically nobody goes to church.

Unfortunately, Catholic life in Latin America suffers from many weak spots. But, absolutely speaking and prescinding from percentages, Latin America is a portion of the Catholic world that possesses much spiritual depth and beauty.

CONTINENTAL CHRISTIAN FAMILY MOVEMENT   One of the institutions which demonstrates this is the Latin American branch of the Christian Family Movement, an organization that has an operating unit in each Latin American nation and that, however limited in its present influence, possesses an admirable program that is lending vitality to Catholic life wherever it operates. Its continental secretariat is based in Montevideo, Uruguay. Its continental presidents are an able and inspiring married couple, Frederico and Hortensia Soneira, who have traveled widely throughout Latin America in the course of their organizational work. Latin American moderator of the C.F.M. is Father Pedro Richards of the Congregation of the Passion who has given powerful impulse to the movement. Father Richards stresses the essential element:

> Many leaders today place emphasis on technology and politics when not on economic measures in the attempt to save this new world of ours. To be sure, these things must be a part of the recuperation.
>
> But at the center must be theology; the figure of Christ must shine in His two redemptions, the redemption of the human person and the redemption of the community. Both missions of Christ are reflected in the miniature world of the family. Here is where the human person is born into the world, is formed for the world, is given a lasting outlook on human living. But he must be truly a Christian when he leaves the home to go into the community. What is not accomplished for the person and for the community in the home can hardly be accomplished outside the home.

The impact of the C.F.M. has been such that the Holy See and the Latin American Bishops' Council have entrusted its leaders with specific tasks, such as the promotion of vocations among youth, the conducting of marriage preparation courses and the encouragement of the wise use of leisure.

The Christian Family Movement is particularly strong in Argentina, Brazil and Mexico. The national directors in Mexico are Senor and Senora Jose Alvarez Icaza, with whom we had a brief encounter at the beginning of this chapter. For the strengthening of the movement in Mexico, Senor Alvarez Icaza has prepared background data for the promotion of the family apostolate not only as it touches Mexico but the entire Latin American world. Further, in order to give proper perspective to this study, Senor Alvarez has introduced comparative data touching family life and social conditions in the United States. His information provides us with a study of family conditions in the Latin American world contrasted with those in our own United States.

CONFRONTATION OF FAMILIES NORTH AND SOUTH   Latin America counts slightly more than 200,000,000 inhabitants and the United States something more than 180,000,000.

True, this approximate equality will not last long since Latin America's population growth is much greater than that of the "colossus of the north." Venezuela, for instance, counts an annual increase of 4.3%. Argentina, at the other extreme, is growing only at the rate of 1.2% per year. Nevertheless the Latin American world registers a general average of 3% annually, the largest continental increase on the globe. The United States increases at the modest rate of 1.7% per year.

Families north and south are not so nearly equal in number. While Latin America counts 40,000,000, the United States reports 55,000,000. This is due to the fact that the average family in Latin America possesses five members while that of the United States averages only 3.4 members. This means that every ten families in the United States has 16 members less than the average ten families in Latin America.

Unfortunately, neither Latin America nor the United States can pride itself on strong family integrity. Experts tell us that matching the United States record for numerous divorces is the prevalence of family disintegration through frequent abandonment of the family by the husband and other forms of family break-up. Of more frequent occurrence than ever, then, in Latin America's social transformation is the non-religious or common law marriage and the diminution of the sacramental marriage.

Thus theology receives a certain melancholy recognition in this common desire both north and south for unstable marriage ties. In the prevalently non-Catholic atmosphere of North America, easy divorce prevails. In a traditionally Catholic Latin America the permanence of the bond of sacramental marriage is recognized; hence the widespread tendency to avoid accepting the bond in the first place or walking out on it rather than following North America's habit of seeking a court decision, even in those countries where divorce is legally possible.

THE FAMILY HOME NORTH AND SOUTH   Basic to every family is the family home. In 1960 the 55 million families in the United States lived in a total of 52 million homes, these homes averaging six rooms each, large and small. A surplus of five million homes in the United States were reported as un-occupied.

In Latin America, instead, the 40 million families possessed 33 million homes with a total of 83 million rooms or an average of two and a half rooms per home. Thus Latin America registers a shortage of 7 million homes for its population and a gross average of 24 persons for every 10 dwelling house rooms in the Latin American world. Thus the statisticians bring home to us the quantitative shortage of residences in Latin America. We can easily understand that Latin American leaders are not exaggerating when they demand the construction of new homes in terms of millions.

Quantitatively, then, homes for Latin American families are in short supply. But qualitatively they are in shorter supply.

Doctor Alvarez Icaza and his confreres offer us Guatemala as an example. This nation of four million inhabitants possesses running water in only 34% of its homes, electricity in 39%, a bath in only 19% and water closets in 29%. A few nations, they explain, are still worse off: The Dominican Republic, Ecuador, Haiti. Slightly better off are El Salvador and Panama. The most advanced so far as its total society is concerned is Costa Rica, small in its population of less than a million and a half but consistently energetic in its provision in many ways for strong family life.

THE PROBLEM OF FEEDING THE FAMILY   Next to housing the family, the most elementary material need is feeding the family. On this score, conditions in Latin America are grave indeed. The Food and Agriculture Organization advocates a world minimum standard of 2700 calories in daily intake. By this measure at least 16 Latin American countries fall below the minimum. Those above the minimum are, in the following order, Argentina, Uruguay, Cuba, Brazil and Mexico. Haiti and Bolivia are the lowest at less than 1900 calories per day. Members of the average family in seven other countries fall more than 500 calories a day below the minimal 2700.

The problem of feeding the family in Latin America is often not one of too little to eat but of the wrong things to eat. Malnutrition means unbalanced diet, lacking animal proteins, vitamins, minerals. It is a problem not merely of money but of age-old habits. Getting millions of parents to teach millions of children to eat unaccustomed food is a formidable task. Three to six of every hundred children suffer from hideous forms of malnutrition. In many areas as many as fifty out of every hundred children suffer from moderate degrees of deficiency. Malnutrition is a continental family problem.

C.F.M. AND THE PUBLIC HEALTH NEEDS   But limiting family concern to malnutrition alone is too narrow. The Christian Family Movement encourages parents to work with the community in the public health needs of every Latin American nation and of the continent as a whole. These needs involve the following:

1. Provision of drinking water and sewage disposal for the 70 percent of the urban population and the 50 percent of the rural population not now properly served in these respects;
2. Reduction of the current excessive mortality among children under five years of age;
3. Eradication of malaria and smallpox and the control of infectious diseases;
4. Better hospitals and family health-care centers in the back country as well as in the cities.

Latin America needs more than 500,000 additional hospital beds and over 100,000 more doctors. With an average of over 400 families dependent on each doctor in the Latin American world, the luxury of a medical man within call is reserved to the favored few among Latin America's families.

EDUCATING THE FAMILY BROOD   The saga of the struggle
of Latin America's millions of families for the education of
their children makes a heart-warming story. The achievement is
still in the process of development since huge numbers of the
population are still illiterate. But during the decade of the
1950's a major phenomenon was achieved, namely, the average middle and lower class family became convinced that its
children should be educated. During the decade of the 1960's
millions of families are seeking to make this a reality.

But to back up this emphasis on more education there must
be money. The fact that 31 million out of 58 million grade
and middle school age children don't go to school is not due
to lack of the will of parents or youngsters to use the schools.
Most often it is because there is no money to build schools.
Very often, it is true, parents must make their youngsters stay
home to help support the household. The economic factor is
the greatest single obstacle to more education in the Latin
American family.

THE DISPARITY IN CLERGY   To terminate this rapid comparison of the Latin American family and its opposite number in
the United States, let us note that as of 1962 the Latin American world was served by 19,064 diocesan clergy and 18,768
clergy of religious congregations, a total of 37,842. In the
United States, to serve 44 million Catholics, less than a fourth
of those in Latin America, 31,961 diocesan clergy and 20,728
priests of religious congregations, a total of 52,689, were available. Thus once again the United States possesses a decided advantage—an average of one priest for each 835 Catholics as
against Latin America's average of one priest for each 4700
Catholics.

A SERIES OF VICIOUS CIRCLES   What conclusion should be
drawn from this series of confrontations in which at practically
every turn we find the Catholic family in Latin America living
and working under handicaps which do not burden to the

same degree the Catholic family in the United States? Senor
Alvarez puts the question this way:

> The Latin American family is faced with a series of
> quandaries that we can well describe as vicious circles:
> 1) For want of material resources a life of virtue is
> difficult; for want of a life of virtue many Latins lack the
> necessary material resources;
> 2) For want of a proper home, of raiment and
> sustenance we do not possess properly integrated fam-
> ilies; and for want of properly integrated families we do
> not possess proper homes, raiment and sustenance;
> 3) For want of proper sanitary facilities we do not
> possess proper living conditions in our homes; and for
> want of proper living conditions in our homes we do not
> possess proper sanitary facilities;
> 4) For want of proper economic resources we are un-
> able to improve our way of life; and for want of proper
> conditions of life we are unable to improve our economic
> resources;
> 5) For want of priests we are unable to possess a
> better Christian family life; and for want of a better
> Christian family life we find ourselves without sufficient
> priests.

SOLUTION: THE FAMILY APOSTOLATE   What is the solution?
In their admirable answer, Senor and Senora Alvarez Icaza
and the thousands of C.F.M. advocates provide us with a new
insight into a deceptively simple instrument which, limited in
development though it be as yet, offers tremendous promise
for the Latin American world.

This answer is the family apostolate.

Some thousands of husbands and wives have clearly recognized the role they can play as lay leaders in Latin America,
have leagued themselves together for service of the community, surely, but always with the definite understanding
that their *primary* task in each case is to build within their own
home a strong Christian family.

Contributing to the continental structure of this movement, the Mexican group notes the importance of the Interamerican Union of Fathers of Families with its seat in Lima, Peru. It recognizes the role of such specialized organizations as the Interamerican Confederation of Catholic Education Associations with its base in Bogota, Colombia.

Of principal importance is the Christian Family Movement which has been most successful in reaching into every country of Latin America. Its beginnings centered in the upper middle class but today it aims to accept families of all classes in each country. Its active membership of some 30,000 families is distributed as follows:

Argentina 8,000; Bolivia 400; Brazil 5,000; Colombia 500; Costa Rica 200; Chile 1500; Ecuador 50; El Salvador 150; Guatemala 150; Honduras 20; Mexico 9,000; Nicaragua 50; Panama 30; Paraguay 150; Peru 400; Puerto Rico 800; Uruguay 1,700; Venezuela 1,500.

PROGRAM FOR LATIN AMERICA'S FAMILIES   Most impressive is the well-balanced and effective program which, though varying in degree from country to country, characterizes the C.F.M. throughout the continent:

1. *Division of information and public relations*   The C.F.M. aims to carry its message both to people of influence in Latin American society and to the general public. It has well-printed bulletins, pamphlets and educational material, radio and television programs and excellently conducted conferences and study clubs.

2. *Division of instruction and formation*   The C.F.M. is notable for its spiritual exercises and retreats for married couples, its discussion groups and conventions, leadership courses on family problems and ideals, vocational promotion and programs to aid seminarians.

3. *Division of public apostolate*   The C.F.M. conducts extensive programs of pre-Cana nature and for the newly

married; programs on family ideals for colleges, parishes and diocesan groups, programs promoting Christian relations between parents and their children, and similar means for promoting family unity.

4. *Division of internal apostolate*   The C.F.M. gives constant attention to strengthening its own organization by gatherings of an administrative nature, financial promotion, coordination of its activities teams. Senor Alvarez describes how it works:

> We dwell ceaselessly on those ideals which represent values so precious for Latin America—the spirit of charity, responsibility, thrift, austerity, industriousness, neighborliness, hospitality.
>
> It is wonderful to see the joy and purposefulness that mark the members old and young of families who have decided together to work for others. Such families may be poor but they join in the fight against the poverty of others, for better food, better houses, better education, better religious instruction. Love of God and of one's neighbor sounds like something very sweet and precious when a child hears his father and mother talk about it.
>
> Soon in many a neighborhood the family that was a lone member of the Christian Family Movement is joined by another family, by four or five others. Thus we grow and this growth will be our finest gift to our beloved brothers and sisters of Latin America.

CHAPTER IX

Doctor Calvani and the Latin American Apostolate

The guests from Latin America at the CICOP conference, prelates, priests and laity, were a distinguished group. Each U.S. citizen who attended the conference came away with memories of his own selected few among them who had made a special impression on him. One outstanding personality was Dr. Aristides Calvani Silva, founder and director of the School of Social Services of the Andres Bello Catholic University of Caracas, Venezuela.

Dr. Calvani has been a lawyer since 1942, a professor and a political leader. But of particular concern to us is the fact that he is a thoughtful student of the Church's apostolate in the broad and deep sense of this term. He probably better than any other speaker from Latin America put his finger most precisely on the requisites which missionaries from the United States should possess for service in Latin America. His message, delivered with a mercurial smile, was truly heart-lifting.

RESPECT FOR OTHER MEN'S CULTURE   "Is not one of the secrets of success of a priest who goes overseas for the Gospel his readiness to adapt himself to the culture of the people among whom he labors? Does not the failure of some missionaries stem from trying to impose their ways on other peoples? Missionaries, for example, sought without success to introduce Christianity to the Chinese in terms of their European customs. It seems that we are successful when we work within the culture of those to whom we go and we usually fail when we become intent upon advocating our own."

Thus at one point of the CICOP conference discussions a priest summarized the current missionary position on culture.

It was for a Latin American layman to surprise the auditors by evidencing his familiarity with this classic missionary controversy of the ages. The layman was Dr. Aristides Calvani of the Catholic Andres Bello University of Caracas, Venezuela.

"This thesis," observed Dr. Calvani, "is ably supported by the splendid book of a Belgian writer on the life of Pere Lebbe of China.[1] Its lesson applies not only to the great world of missions but to Latin America as well. This book made a profound impression on me. It establishes most convincingly the simple fact that the priest succeeds in his apostolate when he approaches with an open mind the persons whom he encounters overseas, seeking first of all to know what these persons are as well as who they are and how they order their lives in the society into which they have been born."

LESSONS FROM ASIA   By the Doctor's reference to Pere Lebbe we are reminded once again of the far-reaching impact which any man may make who dedicates himself wholeheartedly to a great idea. Pere Lebbe was a Belgian Vincentian who reached China in the aftermath of the Boxer Rebellion and who applied the principle of adaptation to his personal life during a period when such a philosophy among missionaries in the Far East had been all but forgotten.

Some outstanding predecessors to Pere Lebbe had voiced this thesis among the missionaries to Asia. St. Francis Xavier had employed the principle of accommodation with brilliant success, as had Robert de Nobili in India and Matteo Ricci in China.

De Nobili, nephew of Cardinal Bellarmine and a relative of Pope Julius III, was sent to India by his Jesuit superiors in 1605. Latourette describes the tremendous handicaps of Christianity through failure of the Europeans to give thought to India's culture. "Christians," he explains, "were regarded by their neighbors as Portuguese and were despised. . . . De-

---

[1] Leclercq, *Thunder in the Distance, the Life of Pere Lebbe*, Sheed and Ward, 1958.

Nobili recognized that some way must be found of ending the identification of Christians with Portuguese."[2] De Nobili proceeded toward this goal by adopting the civil and social customs of an Indian Brahmin. He lived like an Indian holy man, or *sannyasi*, and like an Indian *guru*, or teacher. Despite the hostility of practically all the Europeans, De Nobili met with success and Pope Gregory XV by a bull of 1623 supported his efforts.

Father Matteo Ricci, S.J., entered China in 1583 as a learned mathematician from the West and by careful adaptation to their ways won acceptance among Chinese scholars. De Vaulx explains that "with his tact, learning and virtues Ricci attracted adherents to Catholicism who formed an elite able to see that it was possible to remain Chinese when one had entered the Mystical Body."[3]

THE CHURCH AT HOME AMONG EVERY PEOPLE   The methods of both Ricci and De Nobili were casualties in the unfortunate Asian Rites controversy, but they are respected today for what they teach in this question of accommodation.

In the early years of Pere Lebbe's mission career a parish priest in Paris, Canon Joly, wrote a book on Christianity in the Far East. It was a bitter book which ended by saying that the missionary movement in Asia was bankrupt because of European pride, which could not imagine that other peoples might need to be treated on an equal footing.

This book stirred France and much of Europe to fury and was everywhere condemned. Perre Lebbe recognized its unfortunate maladroitness and took from it just one particular line which he made his own, namely, the assertion that one of the shortcomings in the Far East was the failure to found "a proper native clergy, complete with bishops." Pere Lebbe worked all his life to change this, quietly, respectfully, never

---

[2] Latourette, *Expansion of Christianity*, Vol. III, Harper Brothers, 1939, p. 259.

[3] De Vaulx, *History of the Missions*, Hawthorn, 1961, p. 83.

consciously offending those who disagreed with him. His day of greatest triumph was October 28, 1926, when Pope Pius XI consecrated the first six Chinese bishops at St. Peter's in Rome.

It is most remarkable, as we have already said, that this simple, dedicated priest whose life was lived almost exclusively in China should serve as inspiration to this smiling, gracious university professor of Caracas. And Dr. Calvani's message turns principally around his plea that we of other lands outside Latin America should approach Latin America's peoples, particularly its lowly millions of desperately needy folk, with love and understanding.

THE IMPORTANCE OF ATTITUDE   This is how Dr. Calvani presented the challenge:

> I would like to express the real problem of Latin America. It is this, that all those who live in countries outside Latin America need to recognize one general principle, namely, that, whether they seek to cooperate with Latin America from their homelands or by coming among us, the all-important requisite is their attitude.
>
> First, it is necessary that all high-minded Christians prompted to interest themselves in the plight of Latin America should before all else come to know and accept the Latin Americans as one with them in that they are people, equal with all other peoples before God and human society, possessed in germ with the same nobility of being, partaking of the same human dignity that, despite all passing handicaps, makes them worthy of men's respect and acceptance as their beloved confreres on the planet.
>
> Secondly, in your approach to Latin America's peoples, be sensitive enough not to indulge at first in criticisms and reproaches. To my mind this is very difficult for you to achieve. But it is very necessary for lasting good that on both sides we overlook many, many things.
>
> Thirdly, show your concern not merely for our poverty, for our wretched homes, for our schools, our business

affairs, our faulty governments; show your concern for *us*, for us as people. We are *people*; when all is over and done we wish to be able to say, "They have come to us for ourselves; they wish to be our friends, to be fellow Christians with us, to share God's love with us now and for eternity."

If you would create such sentiments in us the peoples of Latin America would respond most delightedly and most generously in kind. The world would witness the rare spectacle of dwellers on our two continents living together in understanding and true friendship.

THE PLAN FOR A STRONGER CHURCH   There is nothing casual or accidental about the current resurgence of the Church in Latin America. It represents a calculated effort by many magnificent figures in Latin America, clerical and lay, who in their various theaters of action, some large and many quite small, have as of one accord responded to the special needs of the hour. However modest their individual strivings may be, they are achieving a success which awakens the hope that the forces hostile to religion, for a long while seemingly unchallenged, are now being countered.

The movement's more distant origins date back to leaders developed through the Catholic Action programs and similar influences of the 1920's and 1930's. Immediate and tangible causes date from 1955.

Primary credit for this movement belongs to the Holy See, in particular to the person of Pope John XXIII. In its *Notiziaria* for April and June of 1963 the Pontifical Commission for Latin America prints in full in their original language the 33 documents (two from Pope Pius XII and thirty-one from Pope John XXIII) which represent the principal acts of the Papacy in its promotion of the cause of Latin America.

Pope John in the last months of his life made it evident that he rated his labors for Latin America as one of the major realizations of his pontificate, in a category with his efforts for the Ecumenical Council. Near the end, after he had received

Extreme Unction, the dying Pontiff referred constantly to this field of activity by repeating many times, "Oh, the great work for Latin America!" At each utterance his face was transfigured with satisfaction and his hand traced a blessing as if to confirm his words.

THE RIO CONFERENCE OF 1955   The International Eucharistic Congress held in Rio de Janeiro in 1955 played a role in this Catholic revival as it is now frequently called.

This Rio Congress goes into history because when it closed bishops from all the Latin American nations gathered nearby to consider the solemn fact that the plentiful flow of priests that came to Latin America in the past had dried up, that much of the continent was spiritually barren because the Christian millions were no longer properly cared for. This General Conference met from July 25th through August 4th. It was the first and only General Conference of the Latin American hierarchies. The sole previous continental assembly of any kind held by Latin American bishops was the plenary council convoked in Rome by Pope Leo XIII in 1899.

This Rio conference was called by an apostolic letter of Pope Pius XII entitled *Ad Ecclesiam Christi* and dated June 29, 1955. This letter is now viewed as the magna carta of the current revival, the fundamental programmatic document touching the future of Catholicism in Latin America. It is worthy of note that Pope Pius concluded this appeal by making Latin America a responsibility not only of the Latin Americans themselves. "With fatherly concern," he declared, "we address ourselves not only to the prelates and people of Latin America, but to all other peoples, in order that in one way or another each may contribute its own concourse and aid."

CELAM AND THE PONTIFICAL COMMISSION   Out of the Rio general conference came the foundation of an institution that is unique in the Church, namely, the *Consejo Episcopal Latinoamericano*—CELAM. National conferences of the hierarchies of individual nations have long been in operation but here, with a regional secretariat at Bogota, came into being a federation of 17 National Latin American conferences plus a sectional conference representing the hierarchies of the five small Central American countries. The members of the CELAM council were episcopal delegates, one from each Latin American country. This regional entity, unmatched by any similar institution in the Church, concerns itself with some 200,000,000 souls, 35% of the Catholics of the globe.

From Rome the Holy See gave strong support to the Latin American bishops. Even before the Rio conference Pius XII possessed a special committee concerned with the plight of Latin America, which continued to function from 1955 to 1958. On April 19, 1958 His Holiness established the Pontifical Commission for Latin America (CAL) a new curial institution uniting some eight Roman congregations for action in favor of Latin America. The Cardinal Secretary of the Consistorial Congregation is President (now Cardinal Confalonieri) while the Vice-President is the Secretary of the Congregation of Extraordinary Affairs, Archbishop Samore.

The 1963 edition of the *Annuario Pontificio* delineates CAL's functions, stating that it has "the duty to study in its entirety the fundamental problems of Catholic life in Latin America, encouraging close cooperation among the Roman congregations responsible for their solution. It should also follow and sustain CELAM and its general secretariat."

Pope John, who mounted Peter's throne shortly after the establishment of the Pontifical Commission, encouraged the CAL Commission to vigorous action and found in it a ready instrument.

THE ROLE OF POPE JOHN XXIII   Most important of all, however, was the personal activity of the Holy Father himself in the form of Papal letters to the nations.

Pope John addressed a total of nine public letters to the Church in the United States and Canada. Six were sent to the Bishops of Germany commending their assistance. A group of four regarding cooperation with Latin America were addressed to Italy. Letters on the same subject went to Ireland, France, Switzerland, Spain, Holland, Belgium, Malta. His Holiness likewise addressed several letters to conferences of major superiors of men and of women.

The last of all in Pope John's epistolary line was that addressed to the bishops and major religious superiors of the United States, signed with the Pontiff's already feeble hand on April 21, 1963, six weeks before he died. This was a nine page holographic letter which warmly thanked the Church in the United States for its first responses to the Holy See's appeal for personnel for Latin America.

Systematic participation of Canada and the United States dates from the conference held at Georgetown University, Washington, November 2 to 5, 1959. Episcopal committees representing Canada and the United States met with a committee of CELAM representing all Latin America. From this conference resulted the establishment of the Office for Latin American Affairs in Ottawa as center for Canadian activities and the Latin America Bureau in Washington to serve the Church in the United States.

The Church in the United States recognizes a threefold obligation toward Latin America: the provision of personnel, the provision of financial aid and the provision of services.

AN IDEAL FOR OUR RELIGIOUS CONGREGATIONS   At the University of Notre Dame in August of 1961 during a meeting of the major superiors of the religious congregations of the Church in the United States a special representative of the Holy See came from Rome to plead for service of the Church in Latin America. This representative praised highly the work of the priests, Brothers and Sisters dedicated to the Church in the United States and noted the great needs in religious personnel faced by the Church within our borders. Nevertheless, this messenger declared, he brought a call from the Holy See for substantial sacrifices in religious personnel to strengthen the Church in Latin America. The messenger, Msgr. Casoroli, outlined the need:

The judgment and the decision is left to you. However, interpreting the mind of the Pontifical Commission, I offer you an ideal toward which we request every province to strive. This ideal is the following, namely, that each religious province aim to contribute to Latin America in the next ten years a tithe, 10 percent, of its present membership as of this current year. For example, if the present membership is 500, the ideal would be to contribute by the end of this decade fifty members for Latin America.

Naturally, all will not be able to achieve this ideal. But it may be possible to reach at least 90 or 80 percent of it.

For myself, I should like to add one further consideration: in no case should personnel of what might be called inferior quality be set aside for this work. The Church's cause in Latin America requires that your communities make this sacrifice and have the generosity to devote to it some of the best and most qualified of the vocations sent to them by the Lord.

This sequence of unusual events makes abundantly clear the uniqueness of this twentieth century resurgence of the Latin American Church and the beginnings of a reaction throughout those nations of the West in a position to offer cooperation to the Church in the Latin American republics. The Church in the United States is engaged with the rest in making its contribution.

THE MAJOR IMPORTANCE OF PRIESTS   Cardinal Cushing gave this picture of the need for priests:

No matter how we look at Latin America the first and foremost problem from the spiritual viewpoint is the scarcity of priests. The population is increasing more than five times faster than the priesthood, which currently provides only one parish priest for about every 5,000 Catholics. To meet this situation the Church in the United States, despite its own needs, must accept its share of responsibility. Other countries must do the same.

If we are to respond according to our ability to the needs of the Church in Latin America, consider, please, the following:

1. Probably 90 percent of all the energy and money expended by Catholics for the support of their Church is devoted to the preservation of the faith in their parishes or dioceses. But what have we done and what are we doing for the preservation of the faith in Latin America?

2. These countries to the south of our borders, with a population destined to surpass that of the United States, have been peopled by Spaniards and Portuguese who united in marriage with America's Indian stock brought into the Church by explorers and missionaries from Spain and Portugal. In some lands citizens of other European nations augmented the populace. Then, after revolutions brought forth some 20 independent nations, they were left to themselves with gravely inadequate spiritual forces. For some 30 years many were without anӯ bishops.

3. What is the result? Today millions of Latin Americans never see a priest, and millions more wait for years for the sacraments, the channels of grace. Many who possess wealth in abundance have lost contact with the Church and have never been trained to share their abundance with the poor whom they have exploited or with the Church that has the potential to save them from false prophets and dictators.

4. The popes in our times have warned us about the unthinkable possibility of losing millions of Catholics in Latin America to Communism. Pope Pius XII told me to send priests to Latin America. I responded five years ago by founding the Missionary Society of St. James the Apostle for the recruiting of priests who would volunteer, with the permission of their bishops, to go to the poorest of the poor who had no priests or were unable to support them if they were available. Over 100 of them are now located in Peru, Bolivia and Ecuador.

The Pontifical Commission for Latin America was established later by the Holy See. It has been most successful in persuading bishops, religious and missionary superiors to send priests, Sisters and lay apostles to that sector of the western hemisphere. As a result, by 1970 5,000 new priests from other lands should be strengthening the faith of millions of our fellow Christians below the Rio Grande.

DATA ON THE U.S. CONTRIBUTION   The response of the United States to the appeal for personnel for Latin America has been good without being notable. In the two years between January 1, 1962, and January 1, 1964, 761 persons from the United States have entered into the service of the Church in Latin America. Of these 335 (44%) have been Sisters, 212 (27.8%) have been priests and 182 (23.9%) have been lay volunteers.

Today 3512 persons from the United States work for the Church in Latin America, distributed as follows:

Area[4]	Priests	Brothers	Sisters	Scho-lastics	Lay Volunteers
West Indies	350	51	620	14	21
Middle America	319	42	202	6	91
South America	742	109	702	21	222
1964 Totals	1411	202	1524	41	334
1962 Totals	1199	177	1189	34	152
Two Year Gain	212	25	335	7	182

THE HEAVY DIOCESAN CONTRIBUTION   Four religious communities supply 65% of all the U.S. clergy now in Latin America, the Redemptorists, Franciscans, Jesuits and Maryknollers. Very interesting is the fact that as of last January 1st the U.S. diocesan clergy in Latin America represented more than ten percent of the U.S. total. Meanwhile this percentage

---

[4] For fuller data see U.S. *Catholic Overseas Missionary Personnel, January 1, 1964*, Mission Secretariat, NCWC Headquarters, Washington, D.C.

has risen, since every month new dioceses are announcing the assignment of clergy for Latin American service. This spontaneous movement on the part of almost 50 of our total of 140 ordinaries to assume direct responsibility for providing priestly personnel to an area of the Church outside our borders is a phenomenon never before recorded in U.S. ecclesiastical annals. This recognition by so many distinguished American prelates of the grave plight in which their Latin American confreres find themselves is a good augury for greater achievements ahead.

As Cardinal Cushing has pointed out, much attention focuses on the shortage of clergy; writers and speakers refer to a theoretical continental need of 200,000. Many will therefore be disappointed to note that, despite all the attention given the matter, during the last two years the United States has supplied only slightly more than a hundred new priests per year. Our total American clergy in Latin America is 1411, so distributed throughout the continent that only four countries possess more than 100: Brazil has 301, Peru 233, Bolivia 157 and Chile 117. Eight countries have less than 25 each: Argentina, Colombia, Ecuador, Paraguay, Uruguay, Venezuela, El Salvador, Dominican Republic.

CHAPTER X

So You Think You're Ready to Work in Latin America!

Chicago friends and admirers of Father Leo Mahon have come to expect shock treatment when they gather for formal or informal addresses from him, whatever the subject. Somewhere out of the depths of his brilliant mind he draws unexpected considerations that unfailingly succeed in upsetting their equanimity and in propelling them forcefully toward meditation on the basic fundamentals.

Thus the new breed across the United States which for the first time is hearing the call to serve the Church in Latin America can listen to him with great profit. His intention is not to turn them back from their resolve. Rather, he aims to prompt them to take full measure of the task involved in working in Latin America and to take full measure of themselves. With proper respect for the task and proper humility as concerns what they have to offer they can move forward more securely toward the Latin American apostolate.

ATTENTION TO APOSTOLIC METHOD   The thoughtful Catholic interested in cooperation with Latin America will recognize that in addition to the recruitment of precious personnel, attention must be given to the important problems embraced in the methodology of the apostolate, direct and indirect. Wherever earnest missionaries gather there is unending discussion of this subject. Those with a lifetime of experience behind them have their contribution to make; those who approach the subject with a new eye have creative thoughts that often prove precious. In the case of the Latin American apostolate, special care is exercised to seek guidance from the Latin Americans who are at home with the task and the people.

At Chicago the conferees experienced the privilege of dwelling on the insights of one who had the advantage of years of work among Spanish-speaking groups in Chicago fresh from the Latin American orbit. This was Father Leo T. Mahon, now head of the parish of San Miguelito, in the environs of Panama City, the Latin American mission of the Archdiocese of Chicago.

Father Mahon presented this analysis of the needs of the Church in Latin America:

> The task of vitalizing the Church in Latin America is so enormous and so complex that those who want to help must first search for the basic, significant problems and their solutions. To do otherwise would be tantamount to compounding blindness with irresponsibility.
>
> The present Church in North America was helped considerably by the overflowing charity and apostolic spirit of the Church in Europe. Now, as a mature people of God, the North American Church is in a position to exercise this very same charity to our brothers in need in Latin America. But our charity, if it is to be effective, must be both relevant and significant. To put this more concretely, the very complex task of revitalizing or re-establishing the Church in Twentieth Century Latin America involves most, if not all, of the following:
>
> 1. *Creating "family" (community), rather than organization*   The Church, as Christ Incarnate in the world today, is a living, dynamic organism and must never be mere organization. The best of organizations is never of itself Church, nor will it cause Church. The effort must be made to create spiritual family—warm, intimate, loving, self-sacrificial. Once formed, "family" will find its own structure, perhaps heretofore undreamed of structures.
>
> 2. *Building "Church," rather than schools or even churches*   The essence of Church is community of people in Christ. There is a noticeable lack of Christian com-

munity in Latin America today—a lack which thousands of schools, hospitals or temples will not fill. A building, by itself (be it a church, a school or hospital), if it is not the expression of the faith, love and unity of a Christian community, is merely an empty, meaningless, symbol. It would be tragic merely to add more institutions and buildings to the Church in Latin America, already plagued by innumerable, meaningless symbols.

3. *Forming social, rather than merely individual conscience*   The world is fast going collective and is strongly reacting to individualism. Perhaps nowhere is this process so unrelenting and visible as in Latin America. Come it must! But will it come from Jesus, Paul and John XXIII or from Marx, Lenin and Castro?

4. *Forming a saintly people and not merely saints*   We shall all be judged as members of a family, not solely as individuals. In the early, highly collective Church, particular judgment was interpreted in the light of the last day. We must counteract the tendency of the past few centuries to preach the opposite.

5. *Forming a committed, not merely a knowledgeable people*   Our catechetical and preaching methods in the past have too much concentrated on informing people rather than forming them. Academic programs of instruction must give way more and more to formation programs such as Cursillos, Retreats, Better World, and C.F.M.

6. *Focusing the sacraments as encounters with Christ rather than statistical receptions*   Of what value are crowded Masses, full communion rails, long confessional queues, if these same sacraments do not basically change the individual and collective lives of the people? Mere reception of the sacraments, in the light of the condition of the Church in Latin America, would be useless, if not harmful. If necessary for a time, the number of people frequenting the sacraments should be reduced to those who approach them as encounters with Christ, their leader in the battle for Latin America and as a renewal of commitment to Christ in community.

7. *Striving for fulfillment of the law and not mere observance*   The legalistic, minimal preachment of the law

has seriously harmed the Christian dynamic in Latin America. The proper Christian attitude should be one of fulfillment. The true Christian observes the law by rising above it. He does far more in charity than the law requires. The example of Christ, not the Law of Moses, establishes the true pattern for Christian life. Such a standard might possibly reduce, for a time, the number of practicing Catholics, but it would create a dynamic image of Christ in His Church (*the* Sacrament) in Latin America.

8. *Forming Christians in society, not members of Christian societies*   Latin America is moving irrevocably toward a pluralistic culture. The preachment of the Latin American Church, as well as its institutions, has in the past been tied to a unique Catholic culture. Lest the Church become just another interesting relic, it must change its posture and institutions. The Church is no more the end than it is the founder; it is rather the way. We should aim at forming Christians in society—in political parties, in universities, in professions, in unions, and so on, rather than Catholic universities and Catholic unions.

9. *Projecting the faith and not merely protecting it* The call of Pope John to Council sounded the death-knell for "Ghetto Christianity." The Church must never again pretend to be the loaf, the meat, the only light. Rather it must be the leaven that lifts, the salt that savors and preserves, the light that shines brighter than all the rest.

10. *Seeking the truth rather than claiming it*   As Christians we believe that the Truth became Incarnate in humanity. Now we must strive to incarnate, ever more perfectly and ever more relevantly, Christ in our society. This is never an accomplished fact but an ever-continuing process. The truth of the Church lies in Christ. But we shall never possess the fullness of truth—the fullness of Christ—till the last day.

QUALITIES OF THE IDEAL MISSIONARY   For the task as outlined, what should be the qualities of the missionary sent to do the job? Father Mahon proposes a series of eight characteristics. The student of St. Francis Xavier, Matteo Ricci, Robert de Nobili, of the ideas of Pere Lebbe, will read them and note, with due allowance for altered times and circumstances, how well they follow the classic pattern. The priest going to Latin America, Father Mahon suggests, should be:

> 1) A catalyst—not the substance of change; 2) A co-creator—not a functionary; 3) A thought provoker rather than a mere teacher; 4) A revolutionary—not a modernizer; 5) A discoverer rather than an administrator; 6) A brother rather than a father in the Christian family; 7) A man of divine rather than of ecclesiastical faith; 8) A creator of liturgy rather than a mere performer.

LESSONS FOR OUR CHURCH AT HOME   The Church in the United States as it equips itself to serve Latin America and as its members contact Latin America is bound to profit from the impact. Father Mahon gives us his thoughts as to how it will be the gainer:

> It seems to me that if we wish to speak, heart to heart, with Latin American Catholics, we must first learn to speak to ourselves. If we want to understand Latin American Catholics, their strengths, their defects, their potentialities, we must first understand ourselves—North American Catholics, with all our strengths, our defects, and potentialities.
>
> What then are the difficulties of North American Catholicism?
>
> 1. *Weak practice of the Faith*   We are told that only 10% of Latin American Catholics are practicing their Faith, in the usual sense of that term. We are also told that 35% of North American Catholics practice the Faith regularly. Taking into consideration Latin American factors such as enormous distances, lack of education, clergy and facilities, is there as much difference between the scandalously low 10% and disturbingly low 35% figures? To go further—may not the figure of 35% be even more scandalous than the 10%?

2. *Leakage in North American Catholicism*   Are we afraid even to find out how great it is? Is it possible that the defection is disproportionately greater in the lower classes and among the intellectuals—rather than among the middle classes?

3. *Are we so certain that Catholic education is so successful in North America?*   Do not recent surveys tell us that there is no significant difference between the attitudes of Catholic school graduates and those of public school graduates? If this be true, are not our schools, in a sense, a failure also?

4. *We are to be the light of the world and the salt of the earth*   Are our North American Catholics—the well-formed people living in middle-class parishes all over the United States—the shining light and the strong salt of United States society? In the sense of leadership, is there any significant difference between them and their Protestant and Jewish neighbors? Are we producing modern saints and heroes? If so, are we producing more than or as many as our Protestant and Jewish brothers?

It would seem that we can conclude that in the North American Church there are serious defects within our testimony and our commitment to the Word of God. I submit that these defects may well be essentially the same as those extant in the Latin American Church—with one clear difference. Those defects are far more visible and the situation much more urgent in Latin America. The Latin American Church does not have the vast institutions, the large collections, and the numerous personnel to obscure the problem and hide the defects. There the sore is naked for all the world to see. Take the affluence out of North American Catholicism (and thus its middle-class, bourgeois morality) and what would North American Catholicism look like? To change the metaphor, take off the layers of flesh and you may find the same fossilized bone structure!

This is a hard saying, I know, and likely to induce shock. But shock treatment can be therapeutic. Years ago, thank God, I received my first shock of this kind. I had started to work among Puerto Ricans in Chicago. From the start, I liked them very much. However, their Catholicism disturbed me. What seemed to me so important—Mass on Sunday, the sacraments, obedience to law, etc.—seemed to impress them very little. They were far more concerned with *padrinos, fiestas, Santos, novenarios,* burial collections, etc. They professed the same Faith as I but somehow it all came out different.

A LESSON IN TRUE VALUES   His eminence the Archbishop of Chicago had given us a building to be used as a hostel for immigrating single Puerto Rican men. One day a Puerto Rican family came to the building—they had no money and no place to go. The building was already full—so I explained as well as I could and gave them ten dollars. A group of Puerto Rican men who had been working with me (although they hadn't as yet begun to go to Mass), just as soon as the family left, questioned me: "Why did you do that?" Unimpressed by my answer, they told me: "Father, you talk a lot about building a truly Christian community. How are we ever going to do it if you treat people like that? You merely give them money and send them away." My reaction: I was at once ashamed and furious. Because my morality had been attacked?—no, because my value system had been questioned.

This, then, I submit, is what Latin American Catholicism can contribute to North American Catholicism—cultural shock. I, like all other Catholics, believe in God our Father, in His Son sent to redeem us, in His Spirit given to unite us. I further believe He constantly uses the humble to confound the proud, the foolish to confuse the wise. This is what he has done to me through the Latin Americans I have encountered and I firmly believe that, through them, He can do the same for all of us.

How? Those with warm hearts and unjaundiced eyes know that by and large the ordinary Latin Americans are good people. The question can be put thusly. If these people are basically sound and good and believing, and if God's grace is present and sufficient, then why are they not better Christians? Is not the fault ours? Have we, the preachers of the Word, not failed them?

Oh, yes, there are severe obstacles to the preaching of the Word in Latin America. To mention a few:

1) Not enough priests and sisters.

2) Much of church activity is on a quid pro quo basis.

3) We proclaim the universality of the Church—yet many of us in Latin America concentrate on the well-off and ignore the poor.

4) We decry the excessive devotion to Mary and the saints in Latin America but many who decry it use it to fill churches and collection baskets.

I personally, for years now, have worked among Latin Americans both in the United States and Latin America and have not had to work against the goad of the aforementioned obstacles. I would be the first to agree that it is much easier to work unencumbered by such obstacles but we must not fall into the trap of thinking these are the profound problems—dangerous they are, yes, but only superficial. The basic problem with Latin American Catholicism is precisely that the message as many now preach it is dated and increasingly irrelevant. It is so because it is static, individualistic, legalistic, and means-oriented whereas it should be dynamic, collective, idealistic, and eschatological.

DEALING WITH THE RELEVANT   The prepared layman as well as the priest in the United States will read with an eye to his own experience Father Mahon's critique on these four characteristics which he declares represent relevance in Latin American life today:

We must preach a message that is dynamic, collective, idealistic and eschatological. Let us discuss briefly each of these characteristics:

1. *Dynamic vs. Static*   The modern man is motion-conscious—not only the intellectual but also the common man. Everything today is energy, power, motion. Yet we, in our closed world, insist on talking of *states* of grace

and sin. I remember several years ago having a discussion with 40 young Puerto Rican men. They agreed that a man not married by the Church lives in a state of sin. The next point was—"Could a man be in a state of sin and still love God?" One man, echoing the familiar doctrine of the scholastic catechisms said "no." Another immediately jumping to his feet and looking me square in the eye said: "Father, if you say I'm living in the state of sin because I'm not married by the Church—all right, I accept what you say . . . but no one can say I don't love God, my Father, because I do." All the rest of the men were in accord with that position.

State of grace or sin means something to us because we were reared with such static concepts but the common Latin American man was not. To use such terminology is to prejudice our preaching of the Word of God. But grace presented as the power to love, the energy to unite, the motion towards unity—the fire on the earth that Christ mentioned—is very significant to the Latin American, while sin should be explained as the egoistic force in the world, the motion toward disunity, the energy which divides, the power that isolates. The Latin American can never rise to the full stature of the Faith if we continue preaching the Word in a static form. He can not and will not accept it completely and thus he cannot commit himself completely.

2. *Collective vs. Individualistic*   One has only to try explaining original sin in the traditional manner to see blank faces register among Latin Americans. What sense can original sin make to the Latin American if we explain it as some non-culpable individual privation? Yes, he can learn the words but they remain just that—mere words—and as such are obstacles to and not vehicles of total assent. But every Latin American man knows (well, he ought to) what it means to live, to be born into a corrupt and vicious system—a social evil so large and so great it defies curing even by people who themselves are not corrupt. The Latin American understands original sin thus explained and can commit himself to a key truth of the Faith.

3. *Idealism vs. Legalism*   The law of Christianity is love. Jesus did not abrogate the ten commandments—He went further, He preached the idealism of perfection and love—especially in the new commandments, the Beatitudes. To obey the law—because it is the law or in a minimum fashion—is a serious misunderstanding of the dynamic of Christianity. If someone asks me: "Father, If I do this, will it be a mortal or venial sin," I know right away he has missed the whole point of Christianity. We obey because we love—not because we are afraid—nor because it's the law.

Let me give you an example. Not so long ago, during a discussion course, I had several conversations with 22 Panamanian men on the subject of matrimony—only one of whom was married by the Church. Every single man there knew it was the law to be married by a priest; all held themselves to be good Christians but they showed no inclination to rush to the altar. I asked them why they didn't get married by the Church. They replied with the usual stock answers—"It costs too much"; "No priests available." Valid reasons in Panama but superficial. "But," I said, "now that there are priests here who do not charge, why do you not marry?" (Many were not even married civilly.)

Then out came the real reason: "Father, I know you cannot break a Catholic marriage. What would I do if I got married and then my wife left me?" A perfectly reasonable natural fear, against which mere law, no matter what its source, is very weak. But not a Christian attitude, because as Christians—brothers and followers of Christ—we must imitate Christ himself who loved and committed Himself to His wife completely. A Christian means a great lover like Christ Himself . . .

When I finished, I could hear my own breathing, it was so quiet. Then one young man rose and said: "Father, that's beautiful! I never knew that was what marriage meant. Father, I want to get married." One by one they rose and repeated the remark and the resolve. It was easily one of the most thrilling moments of my priestly life. I too had learned something—that while the legal-istic approach does not work with the Latin American, the idealistic does.

I went home that night and read and re-read St. Paul's difficult passages about the Law. All of a sudden they were as clear as falling rain. "I did not know sin until I knew the Law." "The law kills and does not justify." I have yet to meet a Latin American who doesn't know he's supposed to be at Mass on Sunday and be married by the Church. If he doesn't obey, and generally he doesn't, he does not, not because of ignorance, but because of legal-ism which does not motivate sufficiently. If I were to shout in every corner of my parish of San Miguelito that the Law says you must go to Mass—you must be married by the Church—what would be the result? A few, a very few would comply. The vast majority would not because they do not think within a legalistic frame of reference nor are they subject to middle-class morality strictures. The effect, as St. Paul warned me so clearly, would be to drive into them a deeper sense of sin without showing them the way out.

4. *Eschatological vs. Means-oriented*   Closely allied to the first three is our habit of converting, quite illicitly, means into ends, thus ignoring or deemphasizing the true ends. We have been telling North American Catholics for a long time that the good Catholic is the man who goes to Mass on Sunday, is married by the Church, supports his parish, etc.; the fine Catholic is the daily communicant. Try the same thing on the average Latin American and what would be the result? If he likes you, he will accept every word in good humor and proceed to ignore it. If he doesn't like you, he will chalk up one more foolishness on your record.

We go to Mass on Sunday because we want to build a truly Christian community and thus worship God. We go to Communion every day because we need a tre-mendous reservoir of Divine Love with which to unite the world in Christ. One day the Redeemer will come. Those who used all the means, especially the sacraments, to build the kingdom of love and justice, will be on His right side. Everything we say and do, plan and fight for must be in view of that last great Day of Judgment and Unity.

We North American Catholics read the Guardinis, the Rahners, the De Lubacs, the Teilhards—some of us even wade out into the Kierkegaards, the Barths and the Bultmanns—and then we hurry back to Paul and John. But so many of us go right on preaching the Word in a static, individualistic, legalistic manner. We make certain concessions but, for the main, the line remains the same. Because of the circumstances of North American culture, it works to some extent (although, I suspect, to an ever-decreasing extent). But among the masses of Latin Americans, it simply does not work. This then I submit is the great contribution of the Latin American Church to the North American Church—an open confrontation.

CHAPTER XI

The New Laity – South and North

Many of us—and we may include members of the clergy in the number—have never reflected on the possibility that there might be a new laity in at least certain sectors of the Church today. Dr. Calvani of Venezuela states that there is, and in quite fascinating fashion describes its characteristics as he knows it from his work in Latin America.

David O'Shea and others have thoughts on the role which our laity of the United States can play in Latin America.

THE QUALITY OF CATHOLICISM   How does one characterize the quality of Catholicism in Latin America?

Father Tiago Cloin of the Netherlands Redemptorists has served in Brazil since the end of World War II. For a decade he was professor of theology in the major seminary but since 1956 has labored at the national level, latterly in the important post of Secretary General of the Conference of Religious in Rio. He has this comment:

> The quality of Catholicism in Latin America has always intrigued me, particularly because so many are ready to rush in with a shattering generalization that the quality is hopelessly bad.
>
> In West Europe, especially Germany, Belgium, Holland, England and Ireland, and in the United States and Canada, we judge Catholicism by practice. In these countries that I've named, I'd say that the practice is far better than the spirit.
>
> Now let's go to Latin America. As a European I speak for Europe. As an old-timer in Brazil I can speak for

Latin America. In Latin America the practice is far below the spirit.

I would contend that both practice and spirit should figure in judging the quality of Catholicism. Practice of the faith by attendance at Mass and religious devotions shouldn't be higher than the Christian spirit that motivates our daily lives. To my mind, conformity in religious practice is stronger in Europe and North America, though of course I do not deny the presence of much Christian spirit there. But the longer I live in Latin America, the more I become convinced that great numbers of persons who do not and cannot easily attend Mass and devotions, and hence are low on religious practice, live in a truly excellent manner by the Christian ideals that dwell within them and motivate their lives.

I say that if in Holland we had relatively as few priests and religious as have the people today in Latin America. and if in Latin America there were the relatively high percentage of priests and religious as Holland today enjoys, Holland would be a land of pagans and Latin America would be a continent of saints!

LAITY AND SPIRITUAL QUALITY   Dr. Aristides Calvani reminds many people of the high Christian ideals which on examination are found with surprising frequency in Latin America. His revealing analysis of the spirit of the new laity in Latin America provides a view of religious sentiment substantially different from that of the writer or lecturer who declares categorically that Latin American religion is passé.

Dr. Calvani has taught for many years at the Central University in Caracas. When the Andres Bello Catholic University was founded he established its School of Social Sciences in 1959. He has served as legal advisor to the Christian unions of Venezuela since 1951 and was elected to the Venezuelan House of Representatives in 1959 by the Christian Social Party (COPEI). He maintains:

A new laity has been appearing in the world. It has been called a new race. This laity is modifying the face of the Church because of its role in the Church. It helped model the action of the Church on the needs of the world today because the laity is an authentic part of the Church, meant, as is the Church, to serve the world.

Today's layman realizes very well that he participates in the role of the Priesthood of Christ. He is beginning to take responsibility upon his shoulders more and more each day. The layman in Latin America is no exception in this respect, though since Latin America is a vast area his performance is not everywhere the same. We are in the habit of speaking of Latin America as if it were a single whole. But the problems of Latin America vary greatly from country to country and frequently differ enormously within an individual nation. It would be very difficult for me, even impossible, to sum up briefly for you all of the characteristics of our new Latin American laity. I shall try, like an artist, to draw for you the master lines which establish the contours.

THE BROAD LINES OF A CONTINENT   Dr. Calvani seeks to make it clear that the laity of whom he speaks represents no separatist elite:

First, where is this new laity working? In the broad sweep of so many underdeveloped countries, there is considerable diversity. In Mexico and the southern nations of Argentina, Chile, Brazil and Uruguay, society is more mature; but we find vital laymen in the underdeveloped areas as well. This gives us special religious problems because underdevelopment does not refer solely to economics; it involves religion likewise.

As you are well aware, Latin America faces a demographic explosion. Our countries are increasing at the rate of more or less 4% a year. In Venezuela, for example, some 80,000 new workmen seek jobs each year. We possess a birth rate of 45 to 48 per thousand in the country as a whole. There is a great lack of ready material resources and a shortage of capital. Ours is a dualistic society. Unlettered workmen can erect great buildings but they still remain uninstructed and sadly illiterate. Segments of the population in the cities are highly educated and other segments badly underdeveloped. This situation prevails in every country. We have a very emotional religious life, rather than a rational one. It has been said that we prefer an emotional religion to a rational religion.

CHARACTERISTICS GOOD AND BAD   Here now comes harsh self-criticism and a fascinating description of the place of anti-clericalism in Latin American Catholic life:

I would distinguish two categories of characteristics among us. The first are the negative or unsatisfactory ones and the second the positive or favorable.

A word on the negative characteristics: Many times our new Catholic laity is disoriented and confused. We cannot see the woods for the trees. This confusion is one of our prominent characteristics. We would like to do everything at once. We resent very deeply what we resent, but many times it is difficult for us to say precisely what it is that we resent. We lose ourselves in highly diversified action. This brings with it a certain reaction, a lack of coordination and a lack of priorities. We have no time to find the priorities. Hence when we take to action it is very difficult for us to reflect sufficiently to effectively coordinate our efforts. Too often we find ouselves lacking time for reflection.

There is a certain anti-clericalism within our Catholic laity. I wish to be very frank. We may define the clericalization of the Church as the concentration of all the activity of the Church in the hands of the clergy. In this sense, I count myself as anti-clerical too. However, many times this state of mind filters down to two varieties, benign anti-clericalism and harmfully extreme anti-clericalism.

For example, I worked for many years in the labor unions. The unionists, though frankly Christian, resented having a priest present. Thus I have often said that in North America you have no Christian labor unions but you are sometimes more confessional than are we. For instance, in your unions I have many times seen a priest opening the session with prayer. With us, even though we describe our organizations as Christian trade unions, we often have no priest for prayer.

Such an attitude can be explained historically. In Latin America we conserve many vestiges of a materialistic, liberal society. Today our Christian elements fight against this tendency to be anti-religious, but even so these vestiges succeed in keeping us secularist. This explains why sometimes we Christians dedicate ourselves to the apostolate but not in the sense that we count ourselves as working within the Church. Often we wish to work as Christians but not openly with the Church.

LAYMEN WHO SEARCH FOR ANSWERS   Thoughtful men in a society that lacks priests become convinced that they must fend for themselves. Dr. Calvani revealingly explains:

Many problems of a spiritual nature arise from this very important distinction. We consider the spirituality of the laity to be different from the spirituality of the religious. Often we as laymen seek a spirituality for ourselves. Indeed, often we find it in books written for priests or Sisters but nevertheless we regard it as distinct.

For our laymen, for instance, it makes no sense to tell them to be good. "How can I be good?" they'll reply disdainfully. One day a man who was working as a public cleaner asked me, "How can I be a Christian in my job?" I was hard pressed to find an answer for him. This is the dilemma we laymen share. A politician, for example, needs a specifically political spirituality for his job—and where can we find it for him?

Often we have no theologians and I say to myself that we give much too little importance to theology. We need theologians who know well our life during the full twenty-four hours of our day, to give us practical answers and not vague philosophical disquisitions. This is not spirituality. We need answers from the social encyclicals, answers directed from an analytical point of view. We don't find the spirituality which we need.

Many times we face moral problems alone. I can recall instances from my personal experiences as a young lawyer. When I was faced with such problems, I couldn't procure answers from a priest because he possessed no special preparation in the field of law. So I was obliged to arrive at the solutions by myself from my own knowledge. I found myself constantly shifting my position in agitation. One needs preparation in principles. The application of principles needs reflection. But when you have only twenty-four hours in a day and you lack easy access to men trained in principles, it is difficult to meet the situation. The job is so big. The lack of spirituality creates a deficiency within us and we are unprepared for reflection.

MEN ARDENT AND ALERT   When Dr. Calvani speaks about the enthusiasm of Latin American laymen for the apostolate he makes no reservations:

And now as to the positive characteristics in the Latin American: Our layman is generally dynamic and enthusiastic. He is currently very ardent and alert about the apostolate. Day by day he assumes more and more responsibility. He is moved by a spirit of renewal.

Among ourselves we call this a revolutionary mentality. I remarked many times in Europe that we are misunderstood when we speak of revolution. The word for you has a much different connotation than with us. I think it is very important to clarify this. We are revolutionary in the sense that we seek a renewal of all the forms of our society. We are convinced that we can achieve this revolution. Further, we are convinced we have an obligation to carry through this revolution.

We are in the final years of the fight. At this moment we are facing a particularly deceptive world. Venezuela to all appearances is very quiet, but Communism is increasing its subversive war throughout Latin America. I have been studying the situation for two years and in my opinion it is very important for us to know thoroughly the techniques of the war of subversion. This grave situation is the reason why the Catholic laity in Latin America is generally attuned to the social problems. The great problems which we face are social problems. The social character of the problems is what strikes us most.

And they are Christian problems too. When we go to Heaven, we are going to be asked about the food we gave men to eat, the clothes we dispensed, and so forth. The best way to give expression to our lives is not with words. Rather we must give our hearts to others. We must relieve them of their misery.

The manifestations of the presence of this new laity today are found particularly in the socio-economic field. For example, we find a center for development and planning in Chile. We talk more and more about reform of the human structure of factories through the cooperative movement. Similarly we are concerned with industrial plants. We are striving in the direction of the Church's teaching for bettering the condition of the workers inside these factories. Our efforts in Christian unionism really began to count only in 1948. Today we possess a very good union movement in all of Latin America. The Christian social unions in the rural areas are now advancing also though we founded the first international movement in the agrarian zone only a few years ago.

In the religious field the laity possess a number of new movements. I felt very proud during my travels in Europe to encounter many married couples of the Christian Family Movement and to be able to establish a sense of union between our movement in Latin America and the movement throughout the world. As to the political field, you know through the press the strength in Venezuela of the Christian Democratic Party as a great force in the nation. We earnestly desire that its next election will seat the first Christian Democratic president in Latin America. Great hopes lie for us in the universities and in numerous other Christian Democratic fields.

OUR PROGRAM MUST MEET THE TEST   Dr. Calvani has no illusions about the major problem which faces Christianity in Latin America: Given that at some day not too distant, the Latin American world becomes prepared to listen to the protagonists of the Christian program, will our leaders, he asks, supply the solutions that will meet the test?

> But the question remains—shall the Christian program prove able to satisfy modern men's needs? Here again much depends on the theologians. In Germany in 1961 I asked a distinguished theologian the answer to the question of agrarian reform. Agrarian reform requires great sums for financing. If we pay the just price for the land there will be no money to build the new farming society. What do we do? It is a very grave question.
>
> What is the theological answer to the many complex problems of social justice bound up in the major task of adjustment which practically every nation in Latin America must face?
>
> In summary, our Catholic laity is really the hope of Latin America in the fullest sense of the word. Today this laity creates great expectations. The zealous layman is renewing himself in many ways; he is awakening deep desires within himself to serve Latin America well.
>
> We laymen need, then, three things:
>
> 1) Formation more and more—formation to help us distinguish the woods from the trees, the great basic goals as distinct from the petty details;
>
> 2) The theological answers in order to give lay leaders the capacity to judge Latin America's great problems with a Christian mind;
>
> 3) Concrete, practical directives in every field to help us to follow a program of action according to our Christian ideals.

ARCHBISHOP MIRANDA SECONDS THE DOCTOR   The call for theological answers for the great problems of the day drew forth strong approval and commendation from Archbishop Miguel Dario Miranda of Mexico City:

Dr. Calvani sounded an important note when he appealed to the theologians to provide the laity of Latin America with guide-lines for our great commanding tasks.

A generation ago when Pope Pius XI called the laity to play their major role in the Catholic Action movement he likewise turned to the theologians for cooperation. Go, dig into theology, he urged; study the principles involved in the public affairs of our times. Today we can admire the findings which much solid research brought forth and, of course, we recognize great areas still untapped.

In Mexico besides our clergy and Sisters we use 8,000 lay missionaries of the Mexican Church. They labor in numerous fields including even that of preaching, though naturally not from the pulpit. Dr. Calvani mentioned the work in the social, economic, civic, political fields. St. Augustine declared many centuries ago that the best kind of citizen, the best kind of family man, the best kind of public servant comes as fruit of Catholic doctrine. Our laymen of today must up-date these roles.

Guillermo Videla, of the Chilean social action program, added his voice:

Currently in Chile the bishops have given land; but who directs the land reform? Not the bishops but the laymen. Under lay direction we have the Institute of Agrarian Promotion, where skilled technicians play the authentic role of the layman with an agrarian program, a health program, an educational program. The top lay leaders in turn seek for generous Christian cooperation from all lay participants at every level. This matter of land reform is but one instance among a number of important projects of Christian motivation directed in Chile by laymen. Thus in Chile we provide a demonstration of Dr. Calvani's thesis of the new laity.

THE NEW LAITY, U.S. BRAND "And what of the new laity such as we know it among us here in the United States?" in-

quired one of the lay participants at the CICOP Conference.
"What manner of role has it to play in Latin America?" The
answer is constantly sought in lay circles throughout the
country, at meetings such as special sessions held for the Papal
Volunteers on the occasion of the CICOP gathering.

Those best acquainted with Latin America recognize our
United States program as multiform. It goes without saying
that when Dr. Calvani describes the lay thinking in Venezuela
and in Latin America as a whole he is reflecting the rapidly
growing but still minority segment of the upper middle and
lower middle classes. The task of this sector is enormous since
it must hope to influence powerful Catholic elements in the
upper classes and must seek as well to impregnate the tens of
millions of underprivileged. In the colossal task of logistics involved in serving these various elements Latin America's new
laity can rightly welcome apostolic cooperation from European
and North American laymen with a wide variety of talents.

David O'Shea, long a lay leader in the United States and
presently the National Secretary of the Papal Volunteers for
Latin America, offers us a frame of reference which helps our
thinking in this regard:

> What is happening in Latin America today is grimly
> reminiscent of the European industrial revolution, which
> created a working class largely closed to the message of
> the Gospels, and also produced a large middle class for
> whom presence in Church tended to be a mark of re-
> spectability, and piety a private concern with little
> relevance to social issues. The upper class was only too
> willing to support the Church as an instrument of social
> control, with no desire to take an active part personally.
> More dramatically, perhaps, the disruption of traditional
> values and social organization led to a swing toward
> materialistic ideologies which finally found expression in
> Communism, Nazism, and Fascism.
>
> The United States is in many ways a creation of the
> same industrial revolution which precipitated mass mi-
> grations from the European countries. However, this

country has had a different historical experience so far as Catholicism is concerned. Those who came here, especially Catholics, found in their religion a focal point around which to rally in an alien land. This heightened their religious awareness at a time when the appalling experiences of their brothers, who had left the rural areas for European cities, were moving them in an opposite direction—away from religion. By the time ethnic identity was waning in the United States, the great majority were able to move relatively freely up the social scale, actively assisted and encouraged by Church authorities. This again was a different experience from that of their European relatives, including those who went to Latin America. They were long held down by an established class structure which, for example, would effectively deny the children of workers the possibility of anything more than a grade school education.

While historical factors in the Latin American area make its experience quite unique, these contrasting results of industrialization in Europe and in North America point up both the dangers and the opportunities this presents to the Church. Potentials are enormous if the Church moves with the people all the way. If not, disaster is inevitable. Certainly the majority of Church leaders in Latin countries seem determined to help the people usher in a new social order and adapt to its novel challenges and opportunities.

THE NORTH AMERICAN ROLE   Thus in the all-important though specifically restricted area of social issues Mr. O'Shea notes a general parity of experience of the Europeans in North and Latin America. He continues by pointing out a contribution which our laymen may make in this particular area:

It is in this context that Father Roger Vekemans, the Jesuit social scientist active in many phases of the Church's work in Chile, suggests that the mature, well-informed layman from the United States can make a great contribution to the people of Latin America. The North American is a Catholic who has already adjusted

to the demands of life in a rationally organized technological society. He has achieved an integration of his
spiritual life (based on stable and eternal values) with the
needs of his *human* existence where the only constant is
change. Ideally, he understands that to establish a social
order in which there will be no poverty is just as important
as serving the needs of the poor, and that it is precisely
science and technology which make this possible. The
Christian tradition in Latin America, Father Vekemans
feels, needs to undergo what he calls a "cultural mu-
tation," transforming its other-worldly orientation into
a concern for the pressing realities of the here and now,
and a commitment to the concept of human progress.
Men and women from the United States, conscious of
their own heritage, and open to the different and no less
valuable historical experience of the people of the Latin
American area, can be enormously helpful as witnesses
to the potentialities of the Christian life within the frame-
work of technological and pluralistic civilization.

Apart from the generalized role of the North American
in terms of culture—contact and social change, his
presence is requested by Latin American Church leaders
to help them in specific projects. The current distribution
of Papal Volunteers in Latin America by project categories illustrates this well.

LAYMEN IN MISSIONARY APOSTOLATE   Some 30 years before
this current period of strong resurgence of the Church in Latin
America, an organized lay apostolate for service overseas had
come into being in Europe, a rebirth of lay participation in the
missionary apostolate that has existed in the Church in various
forms since apostolic times. Here in the United States several
lay sending societies for overseas service operated their programs, such as the Grail, Loveland, Ohio; the Association for
International Development (AID), Paterson, N.J.; International Catholic Auxiliaries (ICA), Evanston, Ill. The first
diocese to have such a program was Los Angeles. Under the
jurisdictional and financial responsibility of the Archbishop
and the personal initiative of the late Msgr. Anthony Brouwers,

this Archdiocese had launched the Lay Mission Helpers Association.

As an element in the cooperation program of the Holy See, the Pontifical Commission for Latin America on May 19, 1960, approved the establishment of the Papal Volunteers for Apostolic Collaboration in Latin America. The thinking of the Commission was expressed as follows:

1. All those who experience concern for the difficulties which the Church is facing in Latin American countries, are quite aware that the greatest single obstacle is the distressing shortage of priests and religious. Hence the continuous preoccupation of the Pontifical Commission, of CELAM, and of all those concerned with the future of the Catholic religion in Latin America to encourage the inflow of many apostolic workers into those countries.

Unfortunately, although we have obtained some success, there is much more to be done and the number of priests assigned to this important task remains inadequate for the purpose.

2. In this situation no Catholic can consider himself alien to the suffering of the Church, which is a Mother to all. More than ever we can see how appropriate to our times are the words of St. John Chrysostom (In 2 Cor. 18,3,P.G.61, 527): "We cannot place the obligation of every activity of the Church upon the priests; the burden falls upon each one of us in the Church, because each and all of us are members of that one body."

Therefore we must appeal to the laity, who become ever more aware of the desire of the Holy See to see them engaged in the apostolate of cooperation with the hierarchy.

3. It is of paramount importance that laymen be made to understand the necessities of the Church in Latin America and the many problems involved. For the Latin American countries, when restored to the ancient vigor of their Catholic life, will become a reservoir of spiritual energy that will meet not only its own needs but those of many other parts of the world.

4. There is a well-founded hope that selected teams of generous laymen in various countries, in response to the appeal of their bishops, can be organized to volunteer for the service of the Church in Latin America for a given period of years.

These laymen, convinced that "the great hour of the Christian conscience has struck" (Pope Pius XII, Easter, 1948), ready to leave their fatherland and prepared to suffer and to toil for the cause of Christ, deserve the title of "Papal Volunteers for Latin America," and are worthy of association in an organization bearing this title.

PRIMACY OF LATIN AMERICAN LAYMEN   Very important is the care that the Holy See has taken from the beginning that these lay people from abroad should avoid assuming the character of interlopers, stepping uninvited into the jurisdiction of those charged with the burden of the faith in Latin America. The document calls for Latin America's laity to assume primary responsibility for service of the Church, with the laymen from abroad as coordinated cooperators. Time will determine the exact form in which this cooperation will be organized:

5. This call is addressed first of all to the laymen of Latin America, for they, more than all others, must be convinced of the necessity of being united with their bishops to put together their energies, and to establish in every diocese a central nucleus, to which the Volunteers coming from other countries will add the contribution of their work and their support. This enlistment of qualified and well trained laymen will doubtless encourage and accelerate the formation of Christian leaders in Latin America.

The task of the lay volunteers coming from abroad is to work under the direction of the local Ordinaries and in collaboration with the diocesan and national organizations in order to help in training excellent and qualified leaders. In no way shall they take the place of the local leaders.

6. In order that the Papal Volunteers, as they are to be called, may obtain best results, it is necessary that they

be organized in teams, or small groups. The operational
structure of the organization will be the team, which
ensures more favorable living conditions for the Volunteers and better results in the work undertaken. Each
team would be composed of from three to ten members:
entirely of single men, or entirely of single women, or
entirely of married couples.

ORGANIZATIONAL PLAN   Today in the United States the
bishops of 105 archdioceses and dioceses have named PAVLA
diocesan directors who are meant to be primarily responsible
for the promotion of recruitment and for those recruited. Thus
it is evident to the bishops of the United States that this lay
cooperation with Latin America is basically a charge of the
Church itself and not merely the task of generous laymen
operating independently. Four categories of teams are recognized:

1) Teams under the immediate responsibility of the diocesan director;

2) Teams organized by religious communities of men and
women;

3) Teams organized by lay organizations for overseas
service;

4) Teams organized by universities or other special institutions.

The Roman document continues:

It appears that the Catholic groups particularly well
qualified for the recruiting of Volunteers are the various
established Catholic organizations of men and women,
the lay missionary organizations, parishes, colleges, university clubs, and so on. These entities would, as an act of
zeal towards the Church and of solidarity with their
brethren, resolve to organize a team or cooperate with
other groups in organizing one.

7. The enlisting group would assume personal responsibility for each individual enlisted, pay for his

special training, his travel expenses to the field and his return. Furthermore, the enlisting group will keep in touch with the Volunteer during the time he is serving abroad. This period will last from two to five years, with the option to continue longer if the team member so desires.

The requirements for membership in the Papal Volunteers are: a) probity of life, b) teaching knowledge of Catholic doctrine, c) technical knowledge for training leaders, d) acquaintance with Latin-American culture, e) speaking knowledge of either Spanish or Portuguese, f) knowledge of the special activity to which his team is dedicated.

COORDINATING CENTERS Further proof of the close co-operation desired between Latin American Church authorities and PAVLA is the provision in the statement of establishment for national centers of coordination. The Church in Chile has already set up such a national center. For insurance of close cooperation, the PAVLA National Secretariat in Chicago has named three regional field assistants. One in Lima, Peru, will serve the non-Caribbean Spanish language countries of South America, one in Natal will serve Brazil, while a third will serve the Caribbean area. The Pontifical Commission proposes the following on this subject:

8. In each country of Latin America, in accordance with the development of the Papal Volunteers, a national center, depending on the ecclesiastical authority, will be established, whose competency is:
   a) to take care of the enrollment of the local teams;
   b) to negotiate the admittance into the country of the foreign teams, to secure residence, board, operational and travel expenses, and to make their assignment;
   c) to inform the Pontifical Commission of the activities of all groups.
9. Although the precise purpose of the organization is to train Latin American Christian leaders, the Papal

Volunteers may dedicate themselves to various works, according to their qualification and capability, as for instance:

a) Technical teams for catechetical activities, for the training of specialists in the teaching of catechism and the instruction of catechists;

b) Teams of married couples, who will dedicate themselves to spreading the principles of Christian family life, the necessary basis for priestly vocations, and to training leaders in this activity;

c) Technical teams for Catholic Charities activities. Lay experts will train both volunteers and paid staff workers in conducting social centers, house-to-house visitations, etc., on the national, diocesan and parochial levels;

d) Technical teams for urban and industrial problems, to be trained and assigned to heavily Communist areas;

e) Technical teams for rural community betterment, to raise the economic level in backward areas, organize cooperatives and small industries, etc.;

f) Teams for leadership among university students;

g) Technical teams for mass communications activities, such as press, cinema, radio, television, in order to train technicians and local leaders in these fields;

h) Teams for guiding Catholic teachers in public schools. They are needed to train Catholics who are teachers in public schools so that, within the limitations of the law, they can present Christian life and doctrine to their students;

i) Teams for English language teaching, which are highly desired in many countries of Latin America.

PAPAL SUPPORT   The areas of activity of PAVLA candidates are given extensive treatment in the document, which concludes as follows:

10. The Pontifical Commission, which has carefully studied this project, has approved it unanimously, aware

that the organization of the Papal Volunteers can prove a powerful instrument of apostolate in Latin America.

His Holiness Pope John XXIII has deigned to grant His blessing to the undertaking.

Recently Cardinal Meyer of Chicago made the comment, "In looking over Pope John's encyclical *Princeps Pastorum* once again the other day, I was startled by the fact that such a substantial part of it is devoted to emphasizing the necessity of enlisting the cooperation of the laymen."

This is a characteristic experience of both the great and the lowly in Christendom, the sense of surprise that the Papacy has in such categoric fashion called for a new laity. What John proclaimed, Paul has repeated. "We are responsible for our times," our reigning Pontiff declared only recently, "for the life of our brothers. We are responsible for our Christian conscience . . . Now is the hour, the hour of the laity. It is the hour of souls, the hour of those who have understood that to be Christian involves a commitment since they can take part directly in this ministry of salvation."

CHAPTER XII

Methods for the Millions—
A Working Plan
Toward Understanding

The enthusiasm engendered at the CICOP conference prompted many a man present to seek an outlet for his exciting resolutions. Father Vincent Lovett of Kansas City, Missouri, and Father Albert Nevins of Maryknoll ably set forth practical programs for adaptation at every level from the national headquarters to the folksy grassroots community.

Back in the year 1602, a little band of Jesuit missionaries gathered at the town of Salta in what is now Argentina to make plans for their Latin American apostolate. In their records, which are still extant, one of the pregnant conclusions entered on the musty pages is the sentence, "The zeal of the apostle is, like the individual bravery of soldiers, to be subordinated to tactics." Those of us who today continue the planning of the Salta Jesuits may well keep this sentence in mind. The Latin American apostolate deserves the careful subordination of artless zeal to well prepared tactics.

PROPOSALS FROM MEXICO   At the 1964 CICOP conference in Chicago, the group of delegates from Mexico was particularly attentive in listing the outcomes which they felt should follow from the deliberations. Their suggestions are as follows:

1. The textbooks used in North American Catholic schools should be revised to give a truer picture of the peoples and the Church in Latin America. Similar objectives should be set by the Catholic press and other avenues of communications.

2. Adequate measures should be taken to propagate fuller knowledge of Latin America by the various career groups within the Catholic body, the clergy, the religious, the professional men, educators, nurses, social workers, editors, mass membership organizations, and the like.

3. Discussion groups, not too large in size, should be instituted to deal with specific subjects aimed at determining the principles that can promote improved relations.

4. Future CICOP conference programs should be made available well in advance in order that both Latin American and United States participants may come better prepared to the annual assemblies.

5. CICOP should advocate a second program parallel to its own through which Latin Americans would seek to create better understanding of North Americans among the peoples of the great world below the Rio Grande.

A BASIC CHURCH PROGRAM   Thus the Mexicans found themselves thinking along the lines which had prompted the Catholic bishops to initiate the movement which, though for practical purposes it is labeled with the title CICOP, aims to provide a program whereby the mass of Church members in the United States may as Christians achieve fuller understanding, friendship and concern for their fellow Christians of Latin America.

This program should belong to every group of Catholics in the United States. The bishops who initiated this movement will experience a sense of defeat if any religious community, any mass membership organization in the Church assumes that CICOP is a particularistic instrumentality reserved for some special segment of the Catholic body. The CICOP administrative unit possesses the mission under the bishops of the United States of laboring as a service unit, providing the sinews for activating a program which is the property of all who are inspired to employ it to forward Christian understanding in the Western hemisphere.

OPERATION UNDERSTANDING   The Catholic Inter-American Cooperation Program (CICOP) was launched in 1963 by the U.S. Bishops' Committee for Inter-American Cooperation. It aims at mutual understanding and friendship based on the principle that, regardless of social or economic circumstances of life, Christian peoples, indeed all peoples should know and accept each other as people. The program is vital to the Church in the United States in its master plan to recognize its proper relations to the Church in Latin America.

The truth is that most U.S. Catholics, like their fellow-citizens, possess an inadequate understanding of the 200 million Latin Americans with whom they share this hemisphere. In place of facts—historical, social and religious facts—we have too often cherished myths and stereotypes. "The Latins are backward," we hear it said. "They won't practice their religion." "They're lazy!" Such false though all too familiar impressions prevent our coming to grips with the real Latin America. Too often we lack an understanding of how each continent substantially influences the life of the other. This inhibits even our well-intentioned attempts to labor together with the Latin American peoples in resolving the common problems of our hemisphere.

We must find our way out of this fog of misinformation and misunderstanding. We owe it in charity to our Latin neighbors and to ourselves. Their destinies and ours are at stake; the future of our faith and the survival of our way of life are being decided now in Latin America.

Money enters into the matter, but it isn't the answer. It might only become an excuse for withholding the most necessary gift of all, ourselves. Our minds must be penetrated as well as our purses; our hearts stirred as well as our hands.

To make people aware, to make them want to act, to point ways toward effective action, such is CICOP's purpose. Its structure is composed of members of the hierarchy, the clergy, the religious communities, and the laity who know Latin America thoroughly and love it very much and who have dedicated themselves in Christ's name to its cause.

THE PROGRAM FOR UNDERSTANDING   CICOP really began at an unprecedented meeting late in 1959 between a group of U.S. and Canadian bishops and a delegation of bishops from Latin America brought together by the Holy See. Latin needs for material assistance and manpower were frankly discussed, but the visiting bishops asked especially for one thing: that the gulf of misunderstanding separating North America from Latin America be closed and that at long last their peoples be rightly known by their neighbors, especially their Catholic neighbors to the north.

The Subcommittee for Inter-American Cooperation of the U.S. Bishops' Committee for Latin America (a committee of the Catholic bishops of the United States based at the Latin America Bureau, NCWC, Washington, D.C.) set about creating a program specifically designed to promote understanding and friendship and accelerate mutual concern between U.S. and Latin American Catholics. Their program includes:

1. *Annual Inter-American Conference*   An annual international conference presenting the facts of Latin American life, bringing together U.S. and Latin Catholic leaders from various walks of life, and giving them the opportunity to dwell upon the basics—economic, social, cultural, spiritual—which constitute Latin American society.

2. *Local Conferences and Workshops*   Intensive encouragement of regional and local conferences, workshops and "Latin American Days" furthering the work of the national conference and multiplying its effectiveness.

3. *Latin American Studies*   Promotion of Latin American studies in colleges and universities and of educational cooperation of every kind.

4. *Mass Communications*   Diffusion of knowledge about Latin America through every channel of communication and especially through the mass media.

5. *Inter-American Cooperation Week*   To provide a focal period each year during which the various parishes, organizational and educational activities featuring Latin America may be emphasized in special fashion, many bishops and major superiors of the United States advocate the observance of *Inter-American Cooperation Week*.

Inter-American Cooperation Week is the last week in January. During that week every Catholic organization in the United States is asked to hold an observance to promote greater understanding and friendship toward Latin America.

A GOAL FOR ALL CATHOLICS   Thus this movement aims at nothing less than a personal commitment, great or small, by every U.S. Catholic to some form of cooperation with the Church in Latin America. It is not in itself a fund raising movement for Latin America, nor does it seek to provide personnel for work there. It does not, in short, duplicate the good work done by many other organizations, encouraged by the same bishops who advocate CICOP, such as the Papal Volunteers for Latin America.

CICOP has a unique goal essential to the success of all organizations seeking to aid Latin America—stimulating attention, interest and desire for personal commitment to Latin America among all U.S. Catholics. Once true understanding is achieved, friendship will grow, and from that friendship, active moral and material cooperation will flow.

THE POWER OF CAREER GROUPS   As indicated by the Mexican delegates, particular emphasis in this movement for the development of attitudes should be placed in the enlistment of the already established groupings of Catholic society. Speaking in general, the foundation of ad hoc organizations to foster understanding of Latin America does not appear to be advisable; such a practice might lead to a separatist movement that will end by reaching only a small fraction of the Catholic population. True, small units within dioceses for fostering interest in Latin America among all other organizations in the diocese can serve a useful purpose.

The basic principle, however, should be accepted that the CICOP idea is to be communicated to all existing career groups. These groups are in great part covered by the following list:

142 THE CHURCH IN THE NEW LATIN AMERICA

1. The diocesan clergy
2. Religious communities of priests and brothers
3. Religious communities of sisters
4. Grade schools, high schools, colleges, universities
5. Mass membership organizations of men and women, parochial and non-parochial
6. Lay apostolic groups, particularly those such as Papal Volunteers who serve Latin America
7. Professional groups (doctors, lawyers, educators, nurses, social workers, etc.)
8. Business men's associations
9. Youth organizations
10. Organizations for social and economic betterment
11. Newspaper and magazine editors and staff
12. TV, radio and similar mass communications organizations

THE MEANS FOR UNDERSTANDING   What shall be the means whereby this understanding shall be achieved?

Nearest to ideal conditions for coming to know and understand the Latin Americans are attained by living with them. True, individuals have lived within the territory of other peoples for years and yet have failed to come to understand them. Notorious in this respect were the old China hands who lived for generations in Shanghai and other parts and never discovered the true nature of the Chinese. One must be conditioned to know his neighbor wherever in the world we find ourselves.

Nevertheless the few who with right disposition and under proper circumstances live among the Latin Americans are the truly privileged in getting to know them. Most missionaries enjoy this happy experience. Brother Thomas More, Provincial of the Xaverians, succeeded through a relatively short journey of a couple of months.

"Father Darby, president of the Conference of Major Superiors of Men," Brother explains, "led a group of us through ten countries of Latin America. Each of us returned a different person, a different Catholic, a different religious. We saw at first hand the problems about which we talk at home; we met face to face with the people. We lived through the days of the Latin American, which otherwise we of the north comprehend only vaguely by hearsay."

METHODS FOR THE MILLIONS   Conferences such as that conducted by CICOP, at which qualified Latin Americans present the facets of their culture, prove an excellent medium for better understanding. Conferences conducted by North American missionaries and laymen with authentic experience in Latin America can prove very fruitful.

However, for the millions of our Catholics throughout the nation, knowledge and understanding must be communicated by educational agencies, panels and community study clubs, books, lectures, the press and other mass communications agencies. After all, these are the established agencies through which the greater part of all our knowledge and understanding is acquired. Let us take care that means are provided whereby these agencies may be properly informed and then proceed vigorously to employ them.

THE PARISH, A VEHICLE TO UNDERSTANDING   A primary vehicle to this program is the parish. "The use of parish organizations to promote knowledge and understanding of Latin America," Father Vincent Lovett, executive editor of the *Catholic Reporter*, declared at the CICOP conference, "is an important factor in developing the genuinely Christian spirit that will cause our apostolic zeal to overflow into outside-the-parish interests.

"Douglas Hyde has repeatedly stressed the principle that when you make mean little demands on people you get a mean little response, which is all you deserve. If you make a big demand you obtain an heroic response. The pastor who would foster inter-American understanding and cooperation must call upon his parishioners to develop this basic spirit, this prodigality, this love."

OUR PRESS AND OUR SCHOOLS   Of major importance to the effective dissemination of inter-American understanding are adequate services by the press and by our educational systems. Great hopes must be centered in the roles to be played by the Catholic press and our Catholic schools. Father Albert Nevins, M.M., long active in the inculcation of ideas and ideals in the United States, appraised these powerful instruments at the CICOP conference.

"The people of the United States," Father Nevins observes, "have a horizontal approach to history. By that I mean we tend to look right and left on the globe and not up and down. Our main attention becomes focused on Europe and Asia with the result that we tend to take Canada and Latin America for granted. We know a great deal about Paris, London and Rome but very little about Bogota, Lima or Buenos Aires.

"Latin Americans sense this horizontal preoccupation of ours and they resent 'poor cousin' treatment. I am not suggesting that we should forget Europe. Our safety is definitely bound up with Europe. Economically, Europe and Latin America take about equal amounts of our foreign trade. Culturally, Europe takes precedence because our ancestral roots are deep in its soil. But this concern for and interest in Europe should not be at the expense of Latin America, our immediate neighbor."

A SURVEY OF OUR NEGLIGENCE   Father Nevins proposes a quick survey of our recent historical relations with Latin America. Before World War II, President Franklin D. Roosevelt's "Good Neighbor" policy had been very effective. Relations between the United States and Latin America had been warm and intimate. Secretaries of State Cordell Hull and Sumner Welles worked hard for good relationships. The result was that when World War II came, our Latin American neighbors stood by us. Nineteen of the twenty Latin American republics actually put troops in the field to fight alongside us— a fact very few people in the United States remember today.

Then came the end of World War II. The Marshall Plan

directed all our energies to Europe. Massive aid went to European nations to improve standards of living. Latin Americans began to complain that once the war was won, we no longer had need of them. They said that the living standards in Latin America were far worse than those of war battered Europe. They charged that the United States was more interested in its wealthier friends than in its poorest ones.

The United States State Department reflected this European concern. Secretary Dean Acheson and Secretary John Foster Dulles were men who knew Europe, who had European experience. Under their influence the senior diplomatic officers were European-oriented, and one became hard put to find an informed Latin American expert of any authority in the State Department.

REMEDYING THE SITUATION   President Eisenhower attempted to remedy the situation when he sent his brother Milton as his special representative to visit the countries of Latin America. In his report to the President, Dr. Eisenhower observed that there was a lack of knowledge in the United States about Latin America. He made many recommendations in the report about what should be done to bring us closer together.

In 1958 Milton Eisenhower went again to Latin America as the representative of his brother. His report found the same problems he encountered in 1953, only magnified. He spoke of the many misunderstandings that had become "even more serious than they were in 1953." He went on to say: "In the United States, the problem stems primarily from lack of knowledge. . . . our people do not truly comprehend the problems and aspirations of our neighbors, and thus we sometimes take actions which are detrimental to the good relationships we wish to foster."

Once again a report was written but nothing very much happened. Conditions did not change until the election of President Kennedy. He enjoyed a tremendous personal popularity in Latin America, and his Alliance for Progress was a challenging answer to the ills of our neighbors. President Johnson and Secretary Rusk seem to be keeping his spirit alive. But if there has been improvement in government, there has not been much improvement in the realm of education or the press, except by way of exception.

WOEFUL LACK OF KNOWLEDGE "If anyone suspects that the average person in the United States has an abominable knowledge of Latin America," declares Father Nevins, "I can assure him from evidence that he is correct. Recently for my own information, I put together a short questionnaire on Latin America. It consisted of a few questions that would test knowledge—very elementary knowledge. The questionnaire was tried on a group of adults and on a group of teenagers. The scores were almost identical."

Father Nevins' first question was: "When you hear the term Latin America, what is the first thought that comes to your mind?" Here are a few typical answers:

"The tropics. I always wanted to go there."
"Bananas and revolutions."
"Jungles."
"Nothing in particular."
"A place where the rich people won't help the poor people and expect us to do it."
"A mess."
"Brazil. My brother is there."

Another question: "Name one country El Salvador borders." Most did not answer this question. Of those who did, answers were such as:

"Venezuela."
"Mexico."
"None! It's an island."

Only three respondents mentioned either Guatemala or Nicaragua. Particularly revealing was this multiple choice question: "What is the national language of Brazil: Spanish, French, Portuguese, Other?"

33% of the replies said Spanish
11% of the replies said Portuguese
3% of the replies said French
3% said other languages.

DEFECTIVE COMMUNICATION OF KNOWLEDGE   Where does the fault for this lack of knowledge lie? Father Nevins believes that basically it lies in two places—our communications media and our educational curricula. Even those who have some knowledge of Latin America present a view that is highly colored. The editors of *Vision* recently gave forth with some pointed remarks:

> A disturbing attitude towards Latin America has developed in this country. It might be called the "down the drain" syndrome. It manifests itself in a number of ways; glum talk of bankruptcy, flight capital, ballooning inflation, fearful talk of political collapse and chaos, table-thumping talk of Communist takeovers up and down the line. It crops up in business lunches from New York to San Francisco, in government offices, and, most frequently in the press.

"I have spoken to many secular newspapermen about the quantity and quality of material coming from Latin America," Father Nevins notes. "They blame the small quantity on the apathy and indifference of the people of the United States, saying that if the people wanted more news, they would get more. The quality is another story. It is far too much bar stool reporting."

DAMAGE THROUGH FAULTY COMMUNICATION   Venezuela is a case in point. Previous to the recent national elections, U.S. communications media were full of stories of terrorism—bombing of oil lines, arson in U.S. warehouses, bank robberies, kidnappings, and killing of policemen. True, these things happened; and true, they were Castro inspired. True, they should have been reported. But they were not the only things that should have been reported. If one judged by the stories coming from Venezuela, that country was an armed camp of anarchy and terror, where business was being brought to a standstill.

What the press did not tell was the tremendous economic record that was built up over this period by President Betancourt. He led Venezuelans to the highest per capita income in Latin America. In the past year, gross national production of goods and services increased by six per cent. Oil production was up ten per cent. Maracay and Valencia found themselves caught up in an industrial boom, many of the new industries coming from the United States. And at the same time he made a peaceful and democratic transfer of power to his successor.

That is the story that should have been fully told. How many North Americans know that German investment in Latin America has doubled since 1959, is now over 300 million dollars; five times more than its investment in Africa, ten times more than in Asia? Japan has 400 million invested in Latin America, and is increasing at a rate of 25% a year. Who has told this story of confidence and growth?

SMALL INTEREST NETS SMALL COVERAGE   Recently, Pedro Beltran, former prime minister of Peru and ambassador to the United States, came to Miami to give a major policy speech. Although he spoke to editors, coverage was almost nil. Again, Governor Carlos Lacerda of Rio made a major speech in New York on the problems of Brazil and eventual developments there. No New York paper reported the speech. But these are stories that should be told.

We hear about revolutions and coups in Latin America. In 1950, dictators and juntas ruled twelve countries. Today only three dictators remain: Castro in Cuba, Duvalier in Haiti, and Stroessner in Paraguay. Trujillo, Rojas Pinilla, Pérez Jiménez, Somoza, Perón—all had disappeared from the scene. That story has not properly been told. And there are many others: the dynamic young leadership that is coming to the fore; the growing unity of the Latin American hierarchy. These are stories that should be made known to the people of all the Americas.

Outside of the *Diario de las Américas* (a major source of Latin American news in the United States), the New York Times, the Miami Herald, and the Copley News Service, very little interpretive reporting is done. Latin American papers bulge with news from Associated Press and United Press. Latin Americans are being informed about us (and not always accurately) but when will the pendulum swing the other way?

LEAN COVERAGE BY CATHOLIC PAPERS "To demonstrate the lean coverage of Latin American news," explains Father Nevins, "last year I took at random a handful of Catholic papers. I don't mean these conclusions to be final, only indicative. A newspaper which this particular week had nothing on Latin America might at another time have a great deal. But the accompanying table is what I found."

"What does this all add up to?" asks Father Nevins. "I studied 19 papers which contained 24 stories related to Latin America of which only four had any depth or educational value."

A COLUMBIA UNIVERSITY SURVEY A more interesting and accurate survey was made by Father Richard Armstrong, M.M., as part of his work at Columbia's Graduate School of Journalism. Father Armstrong studied 88 Catholic newspapers of the United States for a period of one month, that is for four successive issues. This was a representative study from which definite conclusions can be drawn.

In this one month period NCWC News Service released 150 international stories.

14 on Africa
23 on Asia
19 on Latin America
26 on Europe
22 on Pope.

Paper	Date	Inches	Subject
Catholic Exponent (Toledo)	Sept. 20	0	
Catholic Messenger (Davenport)	Sept. 26	0	
Northwest Progress (Seattle)	Sept. 24	10	Local story diocesan priests in LA, PAVLA
Our Times (Yakima)	Oct. 11	0	
Catholic Virginian	Sept. 20	24	AID couple in Mexico
Los Angeles Tidings	Oct. 11	25	Cuban refugee children
		4	Tito in Mexico (NC)
Michigan Catholic (Detroit)	Sept. 26	0	Third parish to be staffed in Latin America
St. Louis Review	Sept. 27	14	Laity in Latin America
The Anchor (Fall River)	Oct. 17	9	
		17	PAVLA column
		11	Cuban refugee children (NC)
New World (Chicago)	Sept. 27	4	Violence in Colombia (NC)
		24	Bishop Sheen Column
Oklahoma Courier	Oct. 4	19	Reform in LA to overcome Reds (NC)

Paper	Date	Inches	Subject
Universe Bulletin (Cleveland)	Sept. 27	14	Bishop Sheen Column
The Witness (Dubuque)	Oct. 10	0	
Courier Journal (Rochester)	Sept. 20	0	
Observer (Rockford)	Sept. 13	6	Cardinal Ritter on LA (NC)
		26	Gary MacEoin Column
		15	Cardinal Ritter in Bolivia (NC)
Catholic Sentinel	Oct. 10	9	Sister Going to Peru
Monitor (San Francisco)	Sept. 13	24	Gary MacEoin Column
		12	IACI organization
		21	CRS in Colombia (NC)
Providence Visitor	Sept. 13	48	Diocesan priest in Peru
Catholic Standard (Washington)	Sept. 27	36	Interview Bishop McGrath
		15	Cuban Resettlement
		18	Gremillion at Mission Sect. on Alliance
		30	Bishop Sheen Column

The 150 stories amounted to 2,653 column inches. Of the 88 papers only 35 used at least 25% of the material by length.

12 papers over 1,000 inches

Paper	Stories	Inches
Catholic News, NYC	62	1,272
Hartford Transcript	71	1,222
Northwest Progress (Seattle)	54	1,180
Los Angeles Tidings	56	1,105
Saginaw Catholic Weekly	75	1,069
Davenport Catholic Messenger	85	1,067
Newark Advocate	48	1,053
Trenton Monitor	40	1,041
Baltimore Review	58	1,034
Chicago New World	74	1,029
Dubuque Witness	56	1,024
Brooklyn Tablet	51	1,000

Nine papers each used less than 300 inches out of 2,600 furnished. Out of the 625 editorials that appeared in the 88 papers during the survey month only five were on Latin America. The *Catholic News* of New York, Trenton *Monitor*, and Winona *Courier* each had eight international editorials; 16 papers had none at all.

During the month seven syndicated columnists produced 28 columns; only two were on Latin America. During the month only one paper, the La Crosse *Times Review*, reviewed a book on Latin America.

JOB OF THE CATHOLIC PRESS   "Is the Catholic press doing a good job?" queries Father Nevins. "I'd say spotty at best. Five editorials out of 625 does not show any great preoccupation about Latin America. Two columns out of 28 is a better record but hardly demonstrates a conviction that Latin America is of critical concern to our Church and our country."

The year 1964 has witnessed a sharp increase in copy from NCWC News Service and a corresponding increase in the employment of Latin American articles by many Catholic papers.

LATIN AMERICA IN OUR SCHOOLS   "And what about our schools?" asks Father Nevins. "American history is not the history of the Americas but the history of the United States. Geography leaves the student with a smattering of facts, often of the odd and curious. Social studies give no depth of understanding. I spoke to a teacher very interested in Latin America about what was being done.

" 'Actually, the curriculum is so crowded and full now,' he said, 'there is little that can be done. Latin America is always a weak last chapter in our textbooks. I have formed a Latin American club that meets once a week after school. We have over a thousands students here but only twenty show up for club meetings. But you know how much kids read today.'

"This particular teacher has a deep and abiding interest in Latin America. He is trying to do something outside the regular schedule."

PROGRAM FOR PRESS AND CLASSROOM   In view of the critical situation in Latin America and of the need for the people of the United States to understand not only the current situation but, more important, its historical roots, and in order for the people of the United States to know their neighbors to the south, Father Nevins proposes a positive program on the part of press and classroom. It provides an excellent review of the factors involved if widespread knowledge and understanding are to be achieved.

A) GENERAL MEDIA OF COMMUNICATIONS   1) We call on the press syndicates, the newspapers and news magazines which have correspondents in Latin America to strengthen their correspondent corps so that they can give more thorough coverage to Latin America. There is no doubt that these correspondents are one of the major elements in better understanding.

2) We call upon these same press syndicates, newspapers and magazines to concentrate more on depth coverage than on reporting the spectacular. The people of the United States are expected to make judgments and this can only be done by

means of proper evidence presented through the communications media.

3) We call upon the television and radio industry to help remove from the people of the United States the misunderstandings and ignorance concerning our neighbors to the South. Some excellent television documentaries have already been produced but they have been too few and far between. We should like to see a continuing series of public affairs programs which present the full story of each of our southern neighbors; and other programs covering general topics, problems and successes. The 1964 program of the National Council of Catholic Men is an excellent illustration of an effort in this direction.

4) We further call on the communications media which are sending dispatches and programs into the countries of Latin America to realize their responsibility in reporting the intentions and actions of the United States. It will be these same dispatches and programs that will create understanding or misunderstanding of the United States in Latin America.

5) Finally, we call upon all the media of mass communication which send personnel into Latin America to assign their top reporters and personnel to the Latin American scene, and in so doing demonstrate their belief in the importance of this area and the need for outstanding reportage.

B) THE CATHOLIC PRESS   1) In a very specific way, we call upon the Catholic press to develop a unity between the Catholic people of the United States and those of Latin America. There are many theological reasons for such interest and participation which do not need statement here. We should like to see more initiative in obtaining articles on Latin America, more creative journalism in presenting these articles to the American public. We would like to see more interpretive editorials that will bring the American public greater understanding.

2) While NCWC News Service is doing a creditable job under many handicaps, Latin American coverage is uneven. We would like to see the replacement of correspondents who

are not active and creative. We would further like to see a continuing growth in the number and quality of Latin American dispatches serviced by NC.

3) We would like to see developed a regular and continuing series of articles that will interpret Latin America to the Catholics of the United States. We would like to see these articles written by top writers in Latin America. We would further like to see every Catholic newspaper carry these articles.

4) We would encourage Catholic editors and writers to visit Latin America on vacations and assignments. By first-hand visits they will get a greater insight into Latin America, its people and problems.

5) We would like to see the exchange of journalistic personnel on short term basis. This has been done by Catholic Press Association in the past. We would like to see it renewed and expanded.

C) EDUCATION   1) We call upon schools to promote Latin American studies through social science, religion, and other classes. We call for the organization of extra curricular activities that will further develop and practicalize these studies.

2) There has been a trend in recent years on the university level to the formation of inter-American institutes. We would call for the expansion of such institutes, for the teaching and studying of Latin American affairs.

3) We call on primary and secondary schools to set up correspondence exchanges with students in Latin America.

4) We call on universities in the United States to offer mutual cooperation to universities in Latin America. There is a growing interchange between secular universities and Latin American universities, and we would like to see this developed on the Catholic level.

5) We would encourage lecture tours in Latin America by Catholic scholars and artists from the United States, and in the United States by their Latin American counterparts.

6) We would call for an increase in scholarships to deserving Latin American students on the part of foundations

and universities, with freedom on the part of the students to choose U. S. Catholic colleges if they so desire.

7) We would call for an expanded scholarship program on the part of North American businesses that have interests in Latin America.

8) We call upon American families to give lodging to Latin American students in the United States, particularly to assist the NCWC high school program which each year brings many students to the United States for one year.

9) We call upon American families to provide hospitality to foreign students in our midst, and we urge American students to help their fellow students from abroad to fit into American collegiate life and know the true hand of friendship.

10) We would encourage American college students to matriculate at Latin American universities.

11) Finally, we would call upon all Catholic organizations to develop programs related to the history, culture, problems and hopes of the people of Latin America, and to present these programs to their memberships on a continuing basis.

SUPPLEMENT

Latin America in Brief

A ready-reference summary of
social and religious data on
the 20 Latin American nations.

ACKNOWLEDGMENTS

For the preparation of *Latin America in Brief*, acknowledgment is gratefully made to the following:

Rycroft and Clemmer, *A Factual Study of Latin America*, Commission on Ecumenical Mission and Relations, United Presbyterian Church, New York 1963;

Hanson, Harry, Ed., *The World Almanac 1964*, New York World-Telegram and Sun, New York 1964;

Centre Eglise Vivante, Louvain, *Bilan du Monde, Encyclopedie Catholique du Monde Chretien, 1964*, Casterman, Paris;

Inter-American Bank, *Social Progress Trust Fund, Third Annual Report, 1963*, Washington 1964.

Recommendation for further data in this field is made to:

Labelle and Estrada, *Latin America in Maps, Charts and Tables*, Center of Intercultural Formation, Apartado 479, Cuernavaca, Mexico:
Volume I—Socio-Economic Data; handy reference book, graphic and statistical, comprehensive but synthesized, 1963, $10.00;
Volume II—Socio-Religious Data (Catholicism) 1964, $10.00;
Both volumes, $15.00.

Latin America in General

Latin America is composed of 20 nations, each with a people which insists on national identification. Hence under ordinary circumstances it is quite inadequate to speak of particular citizens from the lands to the south as Latin Americans: they desire to be known as Colombians, Peruvians, Brazilians, and so forth.

Of importance also is the fact that the 20 Latin American nations should not be cavalierly tossed into one pot as if they were as similar as a score of large and small potatoes. The individualization goes far beyond the matter of a name. As we return home of an evening, we don't report to the family that we met two interesting "Europeans" during the day. We say we met two Belgians, or Spaniards, or Germans. We are keenly aware of the differences among the peoples of Europe.

We should recognize that despite the employment of only two major languages in the region, there is a similar heterogeneity among the nations of Latin America. There is in many respects as much difference between a Chilean and a Guatemalan as there is between a Norwegian and a Greek. Each nation possesses a long series of distinctive historical, political, religious, cultural and folk values which its citizens prize greatly. These factors of distinctiveness we should seek earnestly to respect.

Father Luis Dolan of the Argentine Passionists bears this out. "I think," he says, "that if we are going to be cooperative we must speak of countries of Latin America rather than Latin America in general. The Communists are not speaking of Latin America. They speak of Panama, of Cuba, of Argentina. They know Panama to the tips of their fingers; they know Cuba to the tips of their fingers. I recently attended a meeting of a Communist group who planned doing something in Argentina.

I was really astounded to see how well they knew Argentina. They really knew my country."

While keeping this distinctiveness clearly in mind, it is quite correct to recognize that there are basic regional characteristics which differentiate the Latin American world from the other geographic and ethnographic grand divisions of our planet.

THE REGIONAL HOMELAND   Latin America possesses an unhappy deployment of its geographic factors. Indeed, no other continent has the combination of such natural disadvantages. While our Rockies are nearly as mighty as the Andes, our western coast possesses the great spread of California and pleasantly livable lowlands to the north. Instead, from Mexico southward to the Strait of Magellan, Latin America's western coastal area is narrow at best. Beginning in northern Peru and extending 1,800 miles to the southern limits of the chemical wastes of the Atacama in northern Chile is desert country with practically never a river whose waters reach the Pacific.

The heart of the United States is the Mississippi Valley. Comparable area in South America is the Amazon Valley. Some day when tropical agriculture is highly developed the Amazon, the prophets tell us, will house a hundred million inhabitants, but for most men today it is a world of fear, bereft of great promise.

All honor, therefore, to the hardy millions who have carved out a homeland in many handicapped regions. Favorable areas exist, such as the marvelous humid pampa of Argentina, beautiful central Chile, the grasslands of Uruguay, the favored provinces of southern Brazil, the intermediate highlands of Peru, Ecuador, Colombia, Venezuela. But the spectacle of so many penniless millions in Latin America is attributable in great part to the unfavorable geographic factors in their dwelling places.

COMMON CHARACTERISTICS OF LATIN AMERICA'S PEOPLE
Compared with North America's Indian peoples, Latin America was favored by superior varieties who developed ancient civilizations that compared well with those on other

continents. Today some 20,000,000 Indians in Latin America still maintain their identity as such. The largest body—over 5,000,000—dwells in Mexico, while a similar concentration is found in Ecuador, Peru and Bolivia. Segments are likewise found in ten other republics.

In the majority of nations, the most distinctive Latin American today is the mestizo. He represents 30% or more in 12 of the republics. Where he predominates, he possesses the deepest sense of belonging; and in many countries he contributes most to building the new middle class. The mestizo totals an approximate 75,000,000 in the Latin American world.

In the temperate lands of southern South America—in Argentina, Uruguay, Chile and southern Brazil—European immigrants have entered in considerable numbers during the last 75 years.

Negroes and mulattoes in Latin America total approximately 35,000,000. The largest concentration is in Brazil, with a second heavy grouping in the coastal areas of Venezuela, Colombia and Ecuador. Haiti, the Negro republic, counts some 4,000,000. The color of his skin does not in itself create a handicap for the Latin American Negro, but he must win social acceptance by education and cultural attainment.

AMERICANS AND LATIN AMERICANS   The Latin American frequently refers to Latin Americans in general as Americans and resents the presumptuousness of citizens of the United States in assuming that the title "American" refers exclusively to the sons of Uncle Sam. True, he has a right to the title; we can only meekly explain that we use it to indicate exclusively a citizen of the United States because the title of our country is so long and clumsy we have no other adjective form for it but "American."

This reference to resentments prompts the reminder to citizens of the United States that, unknown to most of us, the attitude of Latin Americans toward this country suffered a sad decline. All who are interested in proper understanding between the Latin American peoples and our own should be aware of this coolness toward us.

Simón Bolívar referred to the United States as a "singular model of political virtues and moral enlightenment, unique in the history of mankind." This was the general spirit of admiration that prevailed in Latin America toward our nation in the early 19th century. But a sense of unfriendliness has been nurtured to our disadvantage by various forces since Simón Bolívar's day.

An outstanding literary event touching this question was the publication in Uruguay in 1900 of an essay entitled "Ariel," by Enrique Rodó. Rodó makes graceful and noble Ariel the symbol of Hispanoamerican culture and the invisible ogre Caliban the symbol of the insensitive, sensual and stupid culture of the people of the United States. The circumstance that produced "Ariel" was the Spanish-American War, but the essay has been read by virtually all Latin American intellectuals ever since.

In recent years the Communist conspiracy has played its role in blackening our name. Attacks are made on us as capitalists, as protagonists of unprincipled exploiters of the Latin American peasant who grows our coffee and digs our copper. But probably the prime standard argument is the Monroe Doctrine.

To many Latin Americans, explains Gerald Clark, "the Monroe Doctrine is an artifice so designed that the United States can intrude in domestic affairs without giving Latin Americans a chance to summon aid and stand up to intervention."[1]

John A. Crow writes, "Within a period of less than a century, that almost boundless admiration for us turned to resentment and bitter hate. This change in sentiment marks one of the unhappiest chapters in the history of the American hemisphere. It was no sudden about-face, but the result of many years of increasing tension in inter-American affairs."[2]

Here, then, is a huge task in intercontinental fence mending that awaits us.

---

[1] *The Coming Explosion in Latin America*, McKay, 1962, p. 41.

[2] *The Epic of Latin America*, Doubleday, 1946, p. 673.

ARGENTINA
(Republica Argentina)

Area: 1,072,750 square miles. *Population:* 20,990,000 (1963)
Capital: Buenos Aires. *Language:* Spanish

DESCRIPTION   In area, Argentina is the second largest country in Latin
America, next to Brazil. It extends south from Bolivia 2,300 miles
to Cape Horn and from the Andes to the South Atlantic. Most notable
topographical feature in the country is the Humid Pampa, a vast
treeless area with wonderfully rich soil given over to wheat and
cattle raising. Buenos Aires, the capital, is the largest city of Latin
America and ninth in the world (3,700,000).

POPULATION   Argentina counts 19 persons per square mile and thus
is tied with Venezuela as the third most thinly populated nation in
Latin America. Only Bolivia and Paraguay are less dense. The annual population increase is 1.7%; considerably below the 2.6% average
for the South American continent. Only Uruguay is lower. The urban
population is 68%; only Uruguay is higher.
   Argentina's population is composed in substantial part of 19th
century and early 20th century European immigrants. Indians number only 100,000, Negroes and mulattoes 15,000, and mestizos a bare
10%. The life expectancy average is 56.9 years; only Panama and

Uruguay are higher. The country counts 13 doctors and 64 hospital beds per 10,000 population, the best record among all Latin nations for these keys to medical care.

Argentina ranks high in education and culture. Of its children of primary school age, 88% are in school, 30% of those of secondary school age are enrolled and 166,000 attend the Argentine universities. Illiterates in Argentina number only 13.3%, the lowest in all Latin America. The upper middle and lower middle classes in Argentina represent 35% of the population, the largest percentually among Latin American nations. As yet, however, these middle class elements are not notable for leadership.

ECONOMIC FACTORS   The Peron regime (1946-55) proved catastrophic for Argentine economy. Under Peron the nation lost its brilliant world position and has no clear promise at the present moment of regaining it. However, the present per capita income of $799 is the highest in Latin America. It is over $100 higher than that of Western Europe which is $690, though substantially less than the United States ($2,050). The country exports over a billion dollars in goods annually, principally meats, cereals and wool. Argentina, Chile and Venezuela are the only Latin American nations in which agriculture does not contribute the largest share of gross profit. In Argentina manufacturing ranks first.

RELIGION   The Church in Argentina originated through settlements from the West Coast, over the Andes to Cordoba and down from what is now Bolivia to Tucuman. When independence came in 1810 the few priests available were Spanish, politically unacceptable. The Spanish bishop was practically a prisoner when he died in Buenos Aires in 1812. The first post-revolutionary phase represented isolation from both Madrid and Rome. But in 1816 the congress at Tucuman voted for relations with Rome.

This did not, however, prevent Rivadavia, even though a practicing Catholic, from working for a national church in 1824. The mission from Rome of Msgr. Muzzi was not successful. The constitution of 1853 declared the Church dependent on the State and attributed to the State the naming of bishops. In 1884 education was declared lay and the representative of the Holy See was expelled.

In 1897 an accord was reached with Rome. At the turn of the century, however, religious ignorance was rife among the working classes through the absence of spiritual life. Only in the second quarter of the 20th century did better days dawn. Catholic Action was established in 1930 and Pope Pius XI brought about a complete ecclesiastical reorganization. The International Eucharistic Congress in 1934 had important repercussions. Heavy immigration of European

Catholics prompted multiplication of parishes but unfortunately these Europeans did not bring the numerous clergy with them that marked the immigration to North America. Nevertheless, despite the grave handicaps of the past, the Church in Argentina today possesses encouraging vitality.

In 1961 Argentina possessed 46 dioceses and 4,922 priests. This means an average of 4,064 faithful per priest, approximately 25% below the continental average of 5,410. Protestants in Argentina in 1961 numbered 414,333, served by 1,703 Argentines and 500 from abroad.

BOLIVIA
(Republica de Bolivia)

Area: 424,163 square miles. *Population:* 3,950,000 (1963)
Capital: Sucre, the legal; but La Paz, the actual
Language: Spanish, with Quechua and Aymara, the much
   used Indian languages

DESCRIPTION   Bolivia is one of the only two land-locked nations in
Latin America, Paraguay being the second. Paraguay has the advantage
of river connections to the sea. Bolivia is served by a slow-moving
transcontinental railroad from a port in Chile on the west to Sao
Paulo, Brazil, on the east. Actually it possesses the river port of
Guayaramerin on the northern jungle border which, by a three-week
journey through the Amazon Basin, can be reached from the sea.
   Bolivia's chief topographic feature is a great central plateau 12,000
feet high and over 500 miles long lying between two great Andean
ranges which count three of the highest peaks in the Western Hemisphere. La Paz lies in a giant canyon at an altitude of 12,000 feet.

POPULATION   Bolivia has a density of nine, the lowest among the
Latin American countries. Its population growth is 2.4% per year.
Almost half its population (1,660,000) claims pure Indian blood
while over 900,000 more are mestizos. Negroes and mulattoes num-

166

ber 12,000. The country's urban population is 37%, the approximate urban average of eight of the 20 Latin American nations. Life expectancy is 49 years. The country is served by 1.9 doctors and 18 hospital beds for each 10,000 of the population.

Bolivia, while struggling to improve its schools, is currently third highest in Latin America for illiteracy, with 67.9%; almost seven out of every ten inhabitants cannot read. Only Guatemala and Haiti are higher. Now two-thirds of its children of primary school age are in school as well as 11% of those of secondary school age. In 1960 it had 4,000 university students.

SOCIO-ECONOMIC FACTORS The per capita income of Bolivia is $122.30, the lowest in Latin America. In 1960 its exports reached the modest total of $67.9 millions, 65% of which came through tin. Bolivian tin mines supply over 15% of the world market.

Bolivia has been the scene of one of the Latin American efforts toward agrarian reform. The revolution of 1953 relied on the campesino for success. The victors sought action by a six-point program: 1) redistribution of idle land; 2) development of Indian communities; 3) better conditions for agricultural labor; 4) agricultural development; 5) servicing of natural resources; 6) encouragement of migration to undeveloped areas. Leftists in seeking to exploit the reforms so distorted the process that the merits of the original program will never be known. Food production fell off badly and much quarreling marked the peasant movement. But gains were nevertheless obtained in the rupture of an old and evil system.

RELIGION Within half a century of the landing of Columbus a first Christian community was established in what is now Bolivia, not far from Oruro. The Franciscans built up missions in this area during the 16th and 17th centuries.

Meanwhile Spaniards journeyed overland from the present Argentina on the east coast and established a colony in Santa Cruz, now in Eastern Bolivia. The diocese of Santa Cruz was erected in 1605.

As early as 1632 Jesuits attempted work among the elusive and often hostile plains tribes, so different from the mountain Indians. These efforts, which at times cost lives, continued till the expulsion of the Jesuits in 1767. The Santa Cruz clergy were too few to take over the effort, and it was neglected until the year 1930. In 1942 the northernmost area was reorganized and Redemptorist and Maryknoll missionaries introduced.

Independence was declared August 6, 1825. The constitution declared the Catholic Church the state religion but disputes and violence prevailed through almost the entire 19th century. Peace with Church authorities came during the decade of 1888-1898, but a new revolt brought in hostile forces during 1898-1920, which proved very difficult for Church life.

The year 1920 brought better conditions. On May 25, 1925, President Bautista Saavedra officially dedicated Bolivia to the Sacred Heart. In 1931 a Catholic social action congress in Cochabamba resulted in vast plans that were never applied. The Chaco War with Paraguay was partially responsible. Catholic forces worked loyally with the Bolivian army and shared in this disastrous defeat.

In 1942 came reestablishment of religious instruction in the state schools, a measure which was helpful to the degree that Church authorities were able to take advantage of it. Better understanding has characterized Church-State relations in recent years. An accord with the Vatican was signed in 1957 regarding Indian missions and in 1961 the government renounced its right of patronage in the naming of bishops.

Bilan du Monde (1964 edit vol. II p. 154) neatly sums up the present situation:

Civil obstacles to growth of the Church:

1. Lack of minimum living standards for the majority of the people, lack of decent lodging, illiteracy, alcoholism;
2. Illicit unions running to 60-70% illegitimacy in children;
3. Encouragement of Communist theory; lay spirit in anticlerical state officials;
4. Language problems through Indian dialects;
5. Inadequate communications.

Ecclesiastical obstacles:

1. Shortage of clergy; one priest to 5,030 inhabitants;
2. Lack of sacramental life;
3. Prevalence of superstition, revival of ancient cults, ignorance, indifference, all through lack of religious instruction;
4. Impossibly large parishes;
5. Increased pressure of Protestant missions.

Factors of encouragement:

1. Growing vitality of Catholic Action, particularly of the Catholic youth movement;
2. Heightened zeal by the clergy in facing the current problems;
3. Considerable aid through outside clergy.

In 1960 Bolivia possessed 16 ecclesiastical territories with 734 priests, 186 Brothers, 1,066 Sisters.

Protestants in Bolivia in 1961 numbered 46,663, served by 637 Bolivian and 437 foreign personnel.

BRAZIL
(Estados Unidos do Brasil)

Area: 3,287,200 square miles. *Population:* 76,600,000 (1963)
Capital: Brasilia. *Language:* Portuguese

DESCRIPTION   Brazil is the largest nation in Latin America. Compared with the new 50-state United States, Brazil is short an area the
size of Texas of being its equal. The major life of the nation is lived
in the southern quarter of its area focused about the two principal
cities, Sao Paulo (3,674,000) and Rio de Janeiro (3,220,000) but
including as well the ten next largest cities of the nation which vary
in size from Recife with 798,000 to Niteroi with 238,000.

Most distinctive area of Brazil is the watershed of the Amazon River
which roughly includes three-quarters of Brazil. Popular concept
paints the Amazon Valley as a swamp. At flood stage the river is
300 miles wide in spots and creates swamp areas as big as Texas. But
all this inundation, totaling an estimated 23,000 square miles, is less
than one per cent of the Amazon Valley. Ninety-nine per cent of
Amazon country is terra firma. Indeed, two-thirds of all Brazil is
highlands with an altitude from one thousand to five thousand feet.
The future will prove the Amazon's worth to Brazil's people.

POPULATION   Brazil has a density of 20 per square mile. An increase
in density to that of the United States, which currently stands at 50.5,

169

will not tax the potential of its territory. Population increase of Brazil is 2.5% annually. The urban population is 37%. In this respect it differs substantially from the United States, the urban population of which is 69.9%.

Brazil reports 200,000 Indians, less than 1% of the population. Mestizos number 6,725,000, or 9.5%. Negroes and mulattoes total 17,529,000—24.7% of the population. This gives Brazil the major Negro concentration in Latin America. Most Brazilians are free of race prejudice.

Life expectancy in Brazil is 39.3 years for men, 45.5 years for women. Medical assistance in Brazil provides four doctors and 34 hospital beds per 10,000 persons.

Brazil suffers from heavy illiteracy which currently is reported at 50.6%. In its primary schools are 8,014,000 children, which is 80% of the nation's young folks of primary grade years. In its secondary schools are 1,117,000 students, 12% of those of this age spread. There are 93,200 university students. The Brazilian university student today is breaking with the tradition of following exclusively the humanities and liberal arts and is paying greater attention to engineering, science, agriculture and similar fields.

SOCIO-ECONOMIC FACTORS   The official per capita income for Brazil is $374.60. It goes without saying, however, that in a huge country like Brazil, income distribution can be very uneven. Government reports show that the 30% of the population living in the big-business states of the south receive 80% of Brazil's national income. These excessive inequalities represent a major problem for the nation.

Brazil's exports for 1960 reached $1,270,000,000. Coffee comes close to making Brazil a monoculture country since coffee represents 56% of the export trade. Only one other item, cacao, accounted for more than 5% of the total. Brazil produced 60.5% of all Latin American coffee in 1961.

Brazil's middle class has been estimated at 15% of its population, or approximately 12,000,000. For the protagonists of the thesis that Latin America's future lies in strengthening the middle class this is very low. The land tenure problem is an issue in Brazil. One third of Brazil's farms (34.5%) are under 25 acres in size and this one third represents only 1.3% of the total farming land. Only a tenth of one per cent of all the farms in Brazil are over 25,000 acres in size; yet relatively few though they be they possess 19.4% of the nation's farm land. Brazilians contend that bigness is not wrong in itself but becomes wrong if large numbers of men are thereby deprived of their needs.

RELIGION The first Mass in what is now Brazil was celebrated by Father Henry of Coimbra, a Franciscan, on April 26, 1500, near the present city of Bahia. No solid religious foundation was made, however, until the Jesuits under Father Nobrega arrived in 1549. For two centuries priests and missionaries arrived, but either they labored in such fashion that they did not interfere with the program of the Protuguese colonials or they encountered trouble.

Projects, for instance, which would seek to establish reductions (settlements of Indians aimed at betterment of the Indian community independently of the colonists) met with hostility. Every Indian was wanted by the colonists as a laborer; they regarded as nonsense any effort to encourage Indians to establish communities of their own. Toward 1650 a group of Jesuits, despite approval of the Holy See and the King, were expelled from a portion of Brazil for attempting to build a reduction.

In 1759, eight years before their expulsion from Spanish territory, the Jesuits were expelled from Brazil, the work of their arch-enemy Pombal. Diocesan clergy and other religious continued to serve the colonists according as the pattern and the circumstances of the times permitted.

Brazil's independence of Portugal came in 1822. As early as 1808 John of Braganza, the Regent of Portugal, fled to Brazil to escape Napoleon and established the beginnings of an independent regime. Independence actually came in 1822 with recognition by Portugal in 1825.

Amid Brazil's demographic, cultural and economic advances in the 19th century, the Church experienced difficulties from anti-clericalism. Freemasonry, accepted in Brazil during its early stages as so benign that clergy might be Freemasons, was favored by the government and by certain members of the clergy. Two bishops who fought Freemasonry in 1872 were tried and imprisoned.

Peace did not come until the republic was established in 1889. The bishops of Brazil in a pastoral in 1890 noted that the Church under the republic had secured "a certain sum of liberties which she had never succeeded in obtaining during the time of the monarchy." However, substantial growth was not experienced until the second quarter of the 20th century. *Bilan du Monde* (1964, vol. II, p. 168) sums up the weak points and the strong in current Church life:

Geographic obstacles to growth:

1. Immensity of the national territory;
2. Great distances between the major centers;

3. Low population density (11 per square mile in 1950, 20 in 1960);
4. Deficient means of communication.

Social obstacles to growth:

1. Tremendously rapid population increase (31,000,000 in 1927, 70,800,000 in 1960);
2. Extensive internal migration from country to city;
3. Inadequate economic provisions;
4. Unhealthy political movements, "immediatism" in social philosophy, etc.

Religious obstacles to growth:

1. Shortage of clergy, Brothers, Sisters;
2. Religious ignorance;
3. Inadequate sacramental life;
4. Bad distribution of the two-thirds of the population in rural areas which clergy can reach only rarely;
5. Inadequate organization of the laity;
6. Prevalence of superstitious practices;
7. Propaganda methods of some Protestant groups from the United States;
8. Brazilian Freemasonry, Communism, spiritism.

Elements favorable to growth:

1. The tradition of a simple faith deeply rooted in the heart of the Brazilian people;
2. Their keen, generous-spirited character which heightens their natural religious sense;
3. The young and dynamic national episcopate;
4. The current good relations between Church and State, uninfluenced by a concordat or other formalities;
5. Steady growth of Christian educational institutions and of an organized laity;
6. The achievement of new coordination through the conferences of bishops, religious communities and other bodies.

Protestants in Brazil in 1961 numbered 4,071,643, served by 20,546 Brazilian and 1,428 foreign personnel.

CHILE
(Republica de Chile)

Area: 286,400 square miles. *Population:* 8,290,000 (1963)
Capital: Santiago. *Language:* Spanish

DESCRIPTION Chile is described as shaped like a stringbean, stretching 2,630 miles from top to bottom, a greater distance than from Hudson Bay to the Caribbean island of Jamaica. A narrow middle sector represents the hard core of the nation, and here 95 per cent of the population dwell. It includes Santiago, the capital, a city of 1,700,000, important industrial centers and an enchanting countryside.

Northern Chile is among the driest places on earth. Within its hard desert wastes are the rich but forbidding nitrate fields of the Atacama. At the other extreme, southern Chile is one of the rainiest areas in Latin America. Its northern limits have the charm of Scandinavia while the far south is cold and barren, terminated by Tierra del Fuego, an island which counts tiny vestiges of some of the world's most primitive peoples.

POPULATION Chile has an average density of 26, the same as that of Nicaragua. The population increase is 2.4% annually. Two-thirds of the country's population is urban and thus it ranks with Argentina,

173

Uruguay and Venezuela. Chile's mixed bloods total 50% of the population (4,100,000) while its Indians number 130,000. Chile is one of the four Latin American nations that has received large European immigration in the late 19th and 20th centuries. Negroes and mulattoes count 3,500. For medical care there are 6.2 doctors and 50 hospital beds per each 10,000 inhabitants.

Chile holds third place among Latin American nations for a low ratio of illiterates—19.9%. Of its children of primary school age, 86% are in the classroom while attendance at secondary school totals 23.3% of the young people of this age level. University students come to 26,900.

SOCIAL AND ECONOMIC FACTORS   Chile's per capita distribution of national income is $452.90. Thus it stands in the group of five nations whose per capita is above the continental figure of $420.70. Chile's foreign trade is $482.7 million. Again we encounter a nation dependent on a single commodity for its foreign trade, in this case copper; 70.1% of the value of Chilean exports is represented by copper.

Chile's major commodity of export is not agricultural but nevertheless the country has a grave land tenure problem. Its farms of less than 50 acres in size total 62.8 per cent of the country's total; yet the combined area of all these represents but one-fifth of one per cent of the nation's farm lands. On the other hand the farms of 12,000 acres or more, though they number only one-half of one per cent of the total farms, occupy 48% of the farming land of the country.

Chile possesses a relatively large middle class, estimated as 30% of the population. These middle class Chileans are devoted to the education of their children, are alert to the problems of the nation, interested in their homes, wear passably good clothes, serve a modestly good table. Though without the money to dispose of which their corresponding American middle class families possess, they are promising types of what improved living conditions will bring to the middle classes in Latin America.

RELIGION   Spain regarded Chile as its most costly colony. All through the 16th century Chile's Araucanian Indians remained hostile, staging new uprisings after each defeat. To this day the Chilean holds a healthy respect for the fighting record of the Araucanian much as the American does for the record of the Sioux.

Padre Rodrigo Gonzalez Marmolejo was chaplain to Pedro de Valdivia when in 1540 Valdivia began the conquest of what is now Chile. The Church grew up with the colony and when independence came in 1810 Catholicism was accepted as the state religion. Little by little society became more laicized. In 1878 the government took steps of angry reprisal when the Holy See failed to accept its nominee for bishop. Peace was not restored until an able prelate, Monsignor Casanova negotiated an agreement. This same prelate initiated the Plenary Council of Latin America which met in Rome in 1890.

A milestone was passed in 1925 when, in a climate of peace and harmony, Chile and the Vatican agreed amicably on separation of Church and State. Within five years a country which for generations had but three episcopal leaders for its huge domain received 10 new bishops and took on a vitality that has made it a regional Church leader among Latin American countries. Many among the hierarchy, clergy and faithful have sought to transform themselves from traditionally static elements so far as religion is concerned into dynamic participants in a program to serve the Chilean nation. In so doing they have made an impact throughout all Latin America.

While Chileans such as Bishop Larrain of Talca have striven in this direction for more than a quarter of a century, the recent elevation of Cardinal Silva has heightened activities. A Christian socio-economic program delineating the revolutionary changes necessary to enlist the state and private institutions for human betterment has been formulated. The Church's educational effectives in the past 14 years have been augmented by 154% at the primary level and 118% at the secondary level. Rural leadership programs have been highly successful, urban programs less so, but the sum total represents substantial gains. Special groups such as professional men, university students, teachers, nurses and other career groups have become alert Christian participants in public affairs. Radio Chileno has become an outstanding mouthpiece while several periodicals have attained positions of prestigious influence.

The nation now counts 630 parishes, most of them active centers of spiritual life, 2,358 priests (one for every 3,135 Catholics) and 4,558 Sisters.

Protestants in Chile in 1961 numbered 834,839 served by 654 Chilean and 312 foreign personnel.

COLOMBIA
(Republica de Colombia)

Area: 439,513 square miles. *Population:* 16,069,000 (1963)
Capital: Bogota. *Language:* Spanish

DESCRIPTION   Colombia lies in the northwest corner of South America,
extending up the Isthmus of Panama to the Republic of Panama
which once was part of Colombia. Colombia's seacoast on the Pacific
is 913 miles long and that on the Caribbean Sea is 1,094 miles long.

Three great ranges of the Andes run through Colombia from north
to south. These mountains and the high table lands that separate them
represent 30 per cent of Colombia's territory but house 91% of its
population. Bogota, the capital, sits amid mountain grandeur on a
plateau 8,600 feet above sea level. The remaining 9% of the population lives in the other 70% of Colombia's territory, a vast plain land
that constitutes the "back yard" of Colombia, portions of the Orinoco
and Amazon valleys.

POPULATION   Colombia possesses a density of 32 per square mile.
The plains dwellers average in places not more than one per square
mile and thus portions of the rich mountain valleys possess heavy
concentrations of population. Annual population growth is high, 2.9%.

176

The urban population is 48%. Since Panama has 47% urban population and Mexico 50%, these three nations are similar in this respect.

Mestizos in Colombia number 7,392,000 (46%) while Negroes and mulattoes, resident principally in the coastal regions, total 3,150,000 (19.6%). Indians, dwelling principally in the plains, number 150,000.

Life expectancy in Colombia is 48.8 years. The country possesses 4.3 doctors and 32 hospital beds for each 10,000 persons.

Colombia's illiteracy runs to 37.6% of the population. Its primary schools teach 1,674,000 children, 70% of the total children of the corresponding age level. Its secondary schools train 286,000, 14.7% of the young people of the corresponding age level. University students number 22,900. There are 24 universities of which two are Catholic.

SOCIAL AND ECONOMIC FACTORS The per capita distribution of the national income is $373.40. The 1961 export trade had a value of $465,100,000, 71.7% of which represented coffee. An important second commodity is on the increase, namely, petroleum, which during 1961 represented 17.2% of the foreign sales.

For the past 25 years Colombia has operated a program to relieve its agrarian problem. This has consisted in parceling out and colonizing lands belonging to the state as well as private lands purchased from their owners. It has tried, but without great success, to secure financing for this program by a special four-tenths of one per cent tax on landowners.

Colombia counts natural riches but is notorious for its failure to exploit them, particularly its agricultural advantages. It is charged with anti-economic use of its lands, employing rich valley lands for cattle pasturage, because of greater immediate profits in this direction, and carrying on agriculture in mountain areas where the soil is less adapted and where modern methods of mechanization are not possible. Its industrial life is 50 years old and has reached important proportions.

RELIGION The Franciscan Juan de Quevedo, first bishop in what is now Colombia, opened the first religious house in 1514. The coastal city of Santa Marta was the base for expeditions into the interior to establish *encomiendas*, civic-religious institutions aimed at the conversion of the Indians. The missionaries were charged with seeing that the well-being of the Indians was duly considered and frequently there were differences between the clergy and the settlers, whose prime consideration was to see the Indian serve as a laborer. The *encomiendas* were later abolished and the Indians were declared citizens.

At the first synod in Bogota in 1556 reference was made to the numerous Indian conversions. The first seminary was opened in 1582.

Church and State early cooperated in providing education as an auxiliary to Christianization. Several colleges were opened in the early 1600's. The Xaverian University, a major educational institution to this day, was founded in 1622.

As early as 1564 Bogota became the presidency of Spain's various administrative *audiencias*. Settlements on the isthmus of Panama early became of major importance since the gold of Peru and all the wealth from the west coast had to journey by mule back along the "royal road" across the isthmus. Nevertheless Bogota and the New Granada of that day always retained their prestige.

Independence was declared in Bogota, July 10, 1810. While many clergy worked actively with the colonists, the effects of the war on Church and churchmen were calamitous. For over 300 years all religion had depended on the royal patronage; suddenly it was no more. All Church institutions suffered from the long period without bishops. After Bolivar's victory of Boyaca in 1819, the Liberator sought a concordat with the Holy See through the native-born Bishop Lasso de la Vega and the Spanish Bishop Ximenez de Enciso. But despite the opposition of some of the clergy, the colonists insisted on the rights of patronage which the Holy See would not accept. The federated republic of Grand Colombia, founded in 1819, was destroyed in 1826 and Bolivar went sorrowfully to his grave in 1830, with a *modus vivendi* established for neither state nor Church.

Only in 1835 did the Holy See recognize Colombia. The Papal envoy, however, was not accepted by the government and had difficulty entering Bogota. The Colombian government was highly unstable throughout much of the 19th century; there were 70 revolts up to 1903. A frightful uprising in 1879 took 80,000 lives. In 1849 a liberal government attacked the Church; in 1861 and 1876 other persecutions took place. In 1853 Colombia abandoned its claims to the patronage and separation of Church and State was declared. In 1878 religious peace was established and with only infrequent exceptions has since prevailed.

Today Colombia possesses a Catholic life which is for the most part above the general average for Latin America. It counts 51 ecclesiastical territories, 18 of which are in the mission areas of the nation.

Colombia's clergy totals 4,247 of which 2,397 are diocesan clergy and 1,850 religious. This represents one priest per 3,426 Catholics. Colombia's average is 37% above the general continental average of 5,410 Catholics per priest. Some 800 of this clergy are non-Colombian by birth.

Religious Brothers number 2,221 and Sisters total 15,086. Of the 98 congregations of religious women, 27 are Colombian by origin. Catholic educational institutions in Colombia are served by 968 men religious and 6,713 Sisters. In addition to the diocesan clergy, 1,909 men religious are engaged in parochial duties.

Apostolic action in many parts of Colombia is of highly praise-worthy character. A frequently cited example is the Parochial Union of South Bogota, where the clergy of a score of parishes with the collaboration of numerous laity have organized a vital life of the spirit within the worker class of the area.

Most celebrated apostolic institution in Colombia is the Popular Cultural Action, an adult education and socio-economic program initiated by Monsignor Jose Salcedo principally among the moun-taineers of the nation. The work turns about a vast network of radio schools. In 1961 these schools totaled 29,682 serving 681,366 students in 892 parishes. The organization operates Radio Sutatenza, one of the most powerful in Latin America, which transmits to 50,000 spe-cially equipped radio receivers.

Protestants in Colombia in 1961 totaled 92,728 served by 838 Colombian-born ministers and 466 foreign-born ministers. Thus the community averages one minister for every 71 adherents.

COSTA RICA
(Republica de Costa Rica)

Area: 19,653 square miles. *Population:* 1,333,000 (1963)
Capital: San Jose. *Language:* Spanish

DESCRIPTION Costa Rica is the southernmost of the five Central
American republics. It has Nicaragua on its northern border and
Panama, which is not classed as Central American, on its southern
border. Its Caribbean and Pacific coastal areas are tropical but the
major population area in the interior, with an altitude of 4,000 feet,
enjoys a beautiful temperate climate. San Jose, the capital, is midway
between the two coasts; the rail line to Puerto Limon (a port of call
of Columbus on his fourth voyage) is 103 miles, while that to
Puntarenas on the Pacific is 93 miles.

POPULATION Costa Rica possesses a moderately high population
density of 60 per square mile. Its population increase, 3.3% annually,
is the highest of all 20 Latin American republics. The urban population is 36% of the total. Ninety per cent of the population is Spanish.
Mestizos total 80,000 while Negroes and mulattoes, principally
Jamaicans imported for the banana plantations, number 30,118. There
are 2,700 Indians.

Life expectancy in Costa Rica is 54.7 years for the men and 57.1 for the women. Medical care is measured by the presence of 3.9 doctors and 51 hospital beds for each 10,000 persons.

Illiterates in Costa Rica represent 20.6% of the population. Primary school enrollment is 210,000, 60.5% of the age group to be served, while secondary schools train 35,000, 12.6% of the age group concerned. There are 3,000 university students.

SOCIAL AND ECONOMIC FACTORS   The per capita distribution of national income is $361.60, $59.10 below the continental average of $420.70. The total exports in 1961 were valued at $88,300,000. Practically half of this (49.3%) was for coffee while 28% was for bananas. Back in 1871, Minor C. Keith, founder of the United Fruit Company, signed the first concession for a Costa Rican banana plantation. Thanks to relatively strong political and economic stability, Costa Rica enjoys the greatest prosperity among the Central American republics. Unfortunately in 1964 the country suffered gravely from disastrous losses caused by vast deposits of volcanic ash from Mount Poas, an active volcano not far from the capital.

Costa Rica is, with Argentina, Chile and Uruguay, one of the four Latin American republics with a predominantly European population. It has the unique distinction of not being controlled by a landed aristocracy and possesses no large population element suffering from massive indigence. Its government, particularly under President Jose Figueres, has been notable for the promotion of social reforms.

RELIGION   Under the Spanish, Costa Rica belonged to the Captaincy General of Guatemala. It was marked during that period as an area made prosperous through raising the mules employed on the portage road across the Isthmus of Panama. After independence in 1829 the Church enjoyed peace for a considerable period until 1884 when it faced an anti-clerical attack which involved the expulsion of the Jesuits and of the Bishop of San Jose. Some of the anti-Church laws passed at that time were not taken off the books until 1942.

Thanks to well-trained Catholics among the active elements in Costa Rican society, the national social legislation promulgated in 1943 was based on the papal encyclicals. JOC (the Latin American YCW) is active in Costa Rica and in recent years the National Center for Catechetical Education has made strong impact in the way of improved religious education.

Despite the high cultural level and the strong Catholic traditions prevailing in Costa Rica, the Church faces a number of serious obstacles. Most important is the shortage of clergy. The present total of 247 priests represents one for 4554 Catholics. Of these 247, 131 are diocesan clergy and thus primarily responsible for staffing the 88 parishes of the nation. This provides but 15 priests for every 10 parishes which in Costa Rica average 12,000 faithful per parish. Sisters in Costa Rica total 582.

Protestants in Costa Rica count 23,000 adherents ministered to by a personnel of 442, one for each 52 adherents. The stability in Costa Rica prompts the Protestants to use San Jose as regional base. It is the center for their regional radio station, the Voice of the Caribbean.

CUBA
(Republica de Cuba)

Area: 44,286 square miles. *Population:* 6,743,000 (1960)
Capital: Havana. *Language:* Spanish

DESCRIPTION Cuba has traditionally been called the Pearl of the
Antilles. It lies 90 miles off Key West, Florida. It is the largest island
of the West Indies; if laid on the map of the United States it would
extend from New York to Chicago. Havana, the capital, is a brilliant
city with population of over a million and one of the world's finest
harbors.

POPULATION Cuba has a population density of 154 per square mile.
This makes it fourth in line, with Haiti, El Salvador and the Dominican
Republic registering still greater density. Its rate of population increase is 2.0%, low for Latin America. Urbanites in Cuba total 55%
of the population. Life expectancy for men is 50.7 years, for women
56.4 years. Medical care is measured as 9.7 doctors and 23 hospital
beds for each 10,000 persons.

Illiterates in Cuba are 22.1% of the population. Primary school
children total 737,000, which is 47.5% of the total children in this
age group. Secondary school students are 122,000, 8.9% of the related
age group. University students total 24,000.

SOCIAL AND ECONOMIC FACTORS   The per capita distribution of Cuba's national income for 1961 is $516.00, $95.70 above the continental average with only Argentina, Venezuela and Uruguay higher. Its foreign trade for 1961 was $626,700,000; only Venezuela, Brazil, Argentina and Mexico reported higher figures. Major commodity sold was sugar, which accounts for 75.9% of the export value. Tobacco, Cuba's second most important export, represented only a modest 10.1% of the whole.

Sweeping social and economic changes were introduced into Cuba shortly after the 26th of July Movement led by Fidel Castro took over the government on January 1, 1959. The agrarian reform program became effective May 18, 1959. Hundreds of dissidents were executed, moderates were ousted and property was expropriated, including a billion dollars' worth owned by United States interests. Soviet, Communist Chinese and Czechoslovakian economic penetration was invited.

RELIGION   From early in the 16th century the Church worked among the Indians who, through the tragic circumstances of the occupation, soon disappeared. Without satisfactory provision of clergy for the greater part of the long period from the 16th to the early 20th century, the lack of proper administration of the Church on the island left the faithful without vigorous leadership. Reports of the 16th and 17th centuries bear this out. A summary survey of the Church in 1838 speaks disparagingly of the faith as riddled with superstition and poorly developed in the rural areas. In 1868 there was the complaint that the clergy in Cuba (still a Spanish colony) supported Spain despite the widespread call of much of the populace for independence. After independence the people held this against the Church.

Then shortly after 1925 came the rise of Catholic Action, and a consequent rise in religious values among the laity. By the 1950's distinct evidence of a resurgence of the faith in Cuba appeared, led by an excellent young clergy as yet all too few in number. Castro's victory destroyed this. In November, 1960, Castro directly attacked the Church for opposing his communism. In April, 1961, the Cardinal of Havana was forced to take refuge in the Argentine Embassy. June 7, 1961, education was nationalized and the Catholic schools taken over. By the end of the year Bishop Boza Masvidal and 598 priests, 970 Brothers and 2,401 religious had quit the country. Early in 1962 there remained in Cuba 187 priests (78 Cubans, 83 Spanish, 19 Canadians, plus 7 in prison). Catholic activities were not formally suppressed but circumstances did not permit their functioning. Catechetical groups continued to operate, a precious promise of another day.

DOMINICAN REPUBLIC
(Republica Dominicana)

Area: 18,816 square miles. *Population:* 3,333,000 (1963)
Capital: Santo Domingo. *Language:* Spanish

DESCRIPTION   The Dominican Republic occupies the eastern two-thirds of the Caribbean Island of Hispaniola. Christopher Columbus erected a cross on the island high on the Santo Cerro which overlooks the glorious Royal Valley in the heart of the Cibao. Haiti occupies the other third of the island, separated by a border line 241 miles long. Santo Domingo, the capital, is the oldest settlement in the hemisphere. In its ancient cathedral an elaborate tomb contains the reputed ashes of Columbus.

POPULATION   The population density of the Dominican Republic is 160. Its rate of population increase is 3.2%, second only to that of Costa Rica among the 20 republics. The country is predominantly rural with but 28% of its population living in urban areas. Life expectancy is 44 years. The medical care record shows only 1.5 doctors and 27 hospital beds for every 10,000 inhabitants.

The Dominican Republic reports a heavy rate of illiteracy with an average of 57.1%. In its primary schools are 377,000 children, 70% of the nation's total in this age group. In the secondary schools are

22,000 students, a modest 4.4% of the total young people in the corresponding age group. University students number 3,000. The Bishop of Santiago de los Caballeros has made a modest start at founding a Catholic university.

SOCIAL AND ECONOMIC FACTORS The per capita distribution of the national income is $313.20, a figure that is $107.50 below the continental average. The 1961 value of exports was $180,400,000 with sugar the front runner, accounting for 49.6% of the total. Coffee was second in providing 12.5%.

The assassination of General Rafael Trujillo in 1961 after 31 years of terroristic dictatorship found the people of the nation in a difficult state of mind politically and socially. After eight years of occupation by the United States Marines, from 1916 to 1924, there had been but six years of the democratic process before Trujillo took over in 1930. There has been but one normal national election under the provisional constitution of December 30, 1961, followed shortly after by a coup which placed a junta in charge that still rules. It is not surprising that the public should display immaturity in thinking and in common action.

RELIGION The Dominican Republic, even though its current religious leaders bewail the weaknesses of today, can look back to a position of honor which their island played in the beginnings of the faith in the new world. The first missionaries landed here in 1494 and the first diocese was created here in 1511, for which the first bishop was consecrated in 1512. In 1545 Santo Domingo was declared the primatial see of what today we know as the Latin American world.

More important, here on the island of Hispaniola in 1511 the Dominican friar Antonio de Montesinos made his historic plea for justice toward the Indians. "Are these Indians not men?" he cried, "Do they not have rational souls? Are you not obliged to love them as you love yourselves?" Bartolome de Las Casas spent his life thundering forth this cry. "The savage peoples of the earth," Las Casas insisted, "may be compared to uncultivated soil . . . that by labor and cultivation may be made to yield sound and beneficial fruits."

The Church in the area followed an indifferent career during the long period when in Spanish eyes the Caribbean islands were in eclipse compared with the fascinating domains on the southern continent. When the wars of independence came, the island had been conquered by the Haitians, who won their freedom in 1794. It was not until 1844 that the Dominican Republic could be established.

Today there is no question of the authenticity of the faith in the republic though certainly it faces grave problems of instruction and the organization of worship and social action. The five dioceses possess 117 parishes and 283 priests, which means an average of 10,403 faithful per priest and 25,163 per parish. According to the record, only 17 priests per quarter of a million Catholics are engaged in parish work. Fortunately, there is a fairly numerous body of Sisters (829) engaged in teaching, religious formation and works of social action.

Protestants in the Dominican Republic in 1961 numbered 43,765, served by 284 local and 131 foreign personnel.

ECUADOR
(Republica del Ecuador)

Area: 104,500 square miles. *Population:* 4,560,000 (1963)
Capital: Quito. *Language:* Spanish and Indian dialects

DESCRIPTION Ecuador obtains its name from the obvious fact that it lies on the equator; its northern border is 100 miles north of the equator and the southern border is 400 miles south of it. It has Colombia as northern neighbor and Peru to the south and east. Border disputes with Peru have created tension between the two countries. Ecuador feels it has a claim to 77,000 square miles of Amazon Valley territory awarded to Peru by 1942 arbitration.

Ecuador divides into three natural zones. The central highland area, which lies between two ranges of the Andes, is the most important and the pleasantest in which to live. Here the capital, Quito, is located. Second zone is the coastal area, with the port of Guayaquil, a companion city to Quito in national importance. Third zone is the eastern forest and jungle area, in a great portion of which small bodies of Indians of backward culture are found.

POPULATION Ecuador has a population density of 41 while its rate of population increase is 2.8%. A third of its people (34%) live in urban areas. The nation counts 40% of its population as Indian (1,820,000), the majority of whom are mountain stock and Quechua speaking. The mestizo population is 30% (1,370,000). Negroes and mulattoes, found principally in the coastal area, come to 330,000.

The life expectancy averages in Ecuador are 50.4 years for men and 53.7 for the women. Medical care is indicated by 3.4 doctors and 21 hospital beds per 10,000 persons.

Illiteracy in Ecuador is reported as 44.3%. In the primary schools are 579,000 children representing 73.2% of the corresponding age group while in the secondary schools are 67,000 students, 11.2% of the corresponding age group. University students number 6,000.

Ecuador is one of the five countries in Latin America in which more than 20% of the primary school children are in private schools, the majority of which are Catholic institutions. These private schools teach 23% of the children in primary grades. At the secondary school level, 38.9% of the students of the nation are trained in private schools. Further, in various categories of specialized education a heavy portion of the training in Ecuador is in private schools; 22.4% of teacher training, 47% of vocational school training.

SOCIAL AND ECONOMIC FACTORS   Ecuador's per capita distribution of national income is $222.70, a national average which is $268 below the continental average of $420.70. Only Paraguay, Bolivia and Haiti have lower per capita averages. Ecuador's total exports for 1960 came to $104,600,000. Its principal export commodity rates it as a banana republic in that banana sales represent 61.4% of the total trade value. Coffee provides 14.9% and cacao 14.4% of the total. Ecuador was once the principal cacao producer in the world until a crisis in this commodity brought ruin.

RELIGION   The Church was founded in what is now Ecuador early in the 1500's. Evangelization of the Amazon region actually started in that century. Many favorable signs of religious life are revealed in the history of the 18th and 19th centuries, in particular the era of Garcia Moreno. Moreno's extremely benign attitude toward the Church, however, would seem to have heightened the bitterness of the anti-clericals when they eventually gained power. Garcia Moreno arranged the concordat with the Holy See in 1862, favored the Provincial Church Council in 1863, presided at the consecration of Ecuador to the Sacred Heart in 1874.

The revolution of 1895 brought anti-clerical forces to power and hostility toward the Church that prevailed well into the 1900's. A *modus vivendi* was finally arranged in 1937. Today the aggressive antipathies of the end of the century have disappeared and tolerance, even when born of indifference, permits an active program on the part of Catholics.

Ecuador's clergy is of excellent quality. It lives a life of poverty close to the people it serves. There are 1,307 priests, some 200 of whom are foreign born. They average 1 per 3,253 Catholics which is 40% better than the continental average of 5,410. Ecuador's Sisters total 3,222. A great effort toward coordination has been made by Church leaders in recent years with consequent effective programs in social action and education. Since the state provides no subventions direct or indirect for private education, the entire costs must be borne by the faithful.

The evangelization of the non-Christian Indian tribes in the Amazon region is zealously pressed by missionary groups. They number 90, at work in eight different territories.

Protestantism reports from Ecuador the smallest percentual body of adherents in Latin America—11,499 members which is one quarter of one per cent. The Protestant broadcasting station based in Quito, "The Voice of the Andes," is rated as one of the best operated and most effective stations on the continent.

EL SALVADOR
(Republica de El Salvador)

Area: 8,160 square miles. *Population:* 2,666,000 (1963)
Capital: San Salvador. *Language:* Spanish

DESCRIPTION El Salvador is the smallest of the 20 Latin American republics. It is slightly larger than the State of Massachusetts. It is the sole Central American republic with no coastline on the Caribbean since its borders touch only western extremities of Guatemala and Honduras and its shores face the Pacific Ocean.

POPULATION El Salvador has a density of 320, the highest among Latin American nations except for Haiti. Its rate of population increase is 2.7% per year with 35% of its people dwelling in urban areas. Its mestizo stock constitutes 97% of the nation. The average life expectancy for men is 49.9 years and for women 52.4 years. Medical care is measured by an average of 1.8 doctors and 20 hospital beds for each 10,000 persons.

El Salvador's illiterates are 60.6% of the populace which places the country among the half dozen Latin American countries with high rating. Children in the primary schools total 290,000, which is 68.3% of the total children in the nation of that age group. In the secondary schools are 34,000 students, 13% of the corresponding age group. University students number 2,400.

ECONOMIC FACTORS   El Salvador's per capita distribution of the national income is $267.50. This represents $153.20 less than the continental average of $420.70 for the 20 Latin American nations. The value of the nation's exports for 1960 was $116,700,000. Coffee was the major export commodity and represented 69.3% of the total value. Cotton was second, representing 13.5% of the total.

RELIGION   The city of San Salvador was founded in 1539 and served as focal point for the development of the area which today is El Salvador. During colonial days San Salvador ecclesiastically was a dependency of the Diocese of Guatemala. In 1842 after a long controversy on the part of the Archbishop of Guatemala, the Holy See gave El Salvador its own diocese. Through the 19th century El Salvador demonstrated consistent friendliness toward Honduras.

Today El Salvador's most obvious problem is paucity of religious staff. It possesses but 311 priests, which amounts to one per 7,780 faithful. This represents 43.8% greater burden on the Salvadorean clergy than the continental average of 5,410 per priest.

The Church in El Salvador contributes substantially to the operation of schools in the nation. Catholic schools represent only 7% at the primary level but 42% at the secondary level. Catholic teacher training institutes handle 61.5% of the candidates in the nation while 50.2% of the technical school students are Catholic trained.

Protestants in El Salvador in 1961 numbered 57,691, served by 624 Salvadorean and 23 foreign personnel.

GUATEMALA
(Republica de Guatemala)

Area: 42,040 square miles. *Population:* 4,100,000 (1963)
Capital: Guatemala City. *Language:* Spanish and Indian
  tribal tongues

DESCRIPTION Guatemala follows the pattern of most of the countries
of Central America in that it possesses a central highland mass with
lowlands on each of the waterfronts. Its Pacific coastal plain is less
than 30 miles deep and its Caribbean lowlands are a scantily in-
habited wilderness not yet economically integrated into the national
territory.

The bulk of the inhabitants live in the colorful uplands with their
electric-blue skies and foaming milk-white clouds, their bright flowers,
birds and butterflies. Hardly a country in Latin America can match
the costumes and fabrics of the Guatemalan Indian world with its
lovely color combinations.

POPULATION Guatemala's population density is 90 per square mile.
Population growth runs to a rapid 3.1% increase annually, with only
Costa Rica and the Dominican Republic registering a faster increase.
Its urban population is a very modest 20%, with only Haiti lower

among Latin American countries. Mayan Indian stock represents 53%
of the total population and the mestizos 38%. The life expectancy rate
is calculated as 43.8 years. Medical care is measured in terms of 2.1
doctors and 28 hospital beds per each 10,000 of the population.

The illiteracy rate in Guatemala is 70.6%. The enrollment in the
nation's primary schools is 297,000, which is 40% of the total of
739,000 children in the corresponding age group. Secondary school
students number 27,000, or 6% of the 446,000 who make up the corresponding age group. University students total 3,000.

Guatemala is one of the five nation partners in the Plan for
the Regional Integration of Central American Higher Education.
By this plan selected faculties in each university in each country
will be made regional in character and thus serve all five nations.
In Guatemala, as an example, the Faculty of Veterinary Medicine
and Zootechnics has been declared regional and recently received
a grant of $200,000 from the Rockefeller Foundation.

Rafael Landívar Catholic University was founded in Quezaltenango
in November 1961 and has received a grant from the government.

SOCIAL AND ECONOMIC FACTORS   The per capita distribution of the
national income in Guatemala is $267.50, which is $153.20 below the
continental average of $420.70. The 1960 total of exports had a value
of $112,800,000. Of this, 65.8% represented coffee sales and 16.6%
the sale of bananas.

The large Indian population with their prevailing tiny land holdings
make minifundia a socio-economic problem in the nation. Nevertheless
latifundia are also a problem. Farms under 100 acres represent 97.8%
of the total number of holdings but only 27.8% of the actual farm
land. On the other hand, only one tenth of one per cent of Guatemala's
farms are over 5,000 acres in size; yet these embrace 40.8% of the
total farming area.

RELIGION   Guatemala shares with Yucatán in southern Mexico the
distinction of embracing the ancient homeland of the Mayan civilization which, along with the Aztec and the Inca, ranks among the
greatest of the Western Hemisphere. The largest Guatemalan concentration of Mayan descendants is found in the mountain province
of Huehuetenango where 150,000 of these Indians live with 50,000
ladinos, as the modern-living portion of the population is called.

Until very recently, the so-called *costumbre*, a strange syncretism
of old Mayan religious customs and Christian practices, was very widespread in this area. Its prevalence has often been cited as proof that
the Spanish missionary failed. This requires explanation. The Mercedarians, who were the early missionaries here, followed sound tech-

niques; while remolding the spiritual culture of the people in their transition from Mayan practices to Christianity they avoided creating a vacuum by taking care not to destroy completely the old religious ways before properly introducing the new. All would have gone well if the clergy had been numerous enough for a long enough time to provide a steady socio-religious advance. But through outside influence the missionary supply was cut off and a partial retrogression set in. Today's missionaries from the United States have recommenced the process with a program which represents a unique missionary effort in the entire Latin American world.

Guatemala's birth as a republic dates from 1839. Its first government was a dictatorship set up by the Indian Rafael Carrera, a Catholic fanatic who ruled until 1865. A bitter anti-Catholic, Justo Rufino Barrios, operated a dictatorship from 1872 to 1885 and introduced anti-clerical laws which remained on the books until well into the 20th century.

Recent reports give Guatemala 346 priests, an average of one per 10,555 laity, which is almost twice as high as the continental average of 5,410. Among the new forces entering the country are parish clergy from four dioceses of the United States. Brothers number 62 and Sisters 364.

In 1961 Protestants in Guatemala totaled 149,081 while Protestant staff personnel numbered 697.

HAITI
(Republique d'Haiti)

Area: 10,714 square miles. *Population:* 4,390,000 (1963)
Capital: Port-au-Prince. *Language:* French and French Creole

DESCRIPTION   Haiti is a mountainous country which occupies the
western third of the island of Hispaniola in the Caribbean, the sole
French-speaking republic and the sole Negro republic in the Western
Hemisphere. It is a land that has not been gifted with even the minimum of requisites for the full life which men seek. Its area is cut
through with many rivers which run at full flood during the rainy
season and are virtually dry the greater part of the year. It counts
few and paltry natural resources: 43% of its area is sterile and un-
usable and only one third can be cultivated. Its minerals are few and
not sufficiently rich to attract the investor. Its forests have been over-cut
and for want of their protection the land is badly eroded.

POPULATION   Haiti has the highest density of all Latin American
nations—327 per square mile. Its rate of population increase is 2.2%.
Its urban population is 17%, the lowest in the Latin American world.
Life expectancy is 32.6 years.

Haiti's illiteracy is 89.5%, the highest among the Latin American
nations. Children in primary school are reported by UNESCO as
238,000, which is 36.5% of the corresponding age group. Secondary

196

school students number 19,000, or 3.2% of the corresponding age group of 563,000. There are 900 university students.

SOCIAL AND ECONOMIC FACTORS   The per capita distribution of the national income is $149.20, next to Bolivia the lowest in the Americas. It is $271.50 below the continental average for Latin America. The export total for 1960 was $38,400,000. The top sales item was coffee which accounts for 55.5% of the total with sisal accounting for 12.2%.

An inhuman system under which 40,000 whites profited from the labors of 400,000 Negro slaves set the scene for the birth of the Haitian Republic. During the 18th century French Haiti enjoyed unbelievable prosperity. But in 1791 the Negroes revolted. Definitive independence came January 1, 1804. However, seldom in the past 160 years has a smoothly functioning democratic regime existed. The present Duvalier government has been in conflict with the Church as well as with its political enemies.

RELIGION   The area now called Haiti shared its life of religion during the early years with the main part of the island though often politically opposed regimes occupied the respective divisions. In 1872 a seminary to supply clergy for Haiti was opened in Nantes, France, which in 22 years supplied 196 priests to the Haitian people. In 1894 this initiative was transferred to the Diocese of Quimper, France; in 28 years 220 priests were supplied. In 1948 the Jesuits opened a seminary for Haitian candidates.

In works of charity the Church has cooperated with the State by staffing hospitals, dispensaries and asylums. In an important number of cases such institutions have originated through funds from abroad. Certain institutions such as orphanages and shelters have been supported by public charity. During the last 30 years there have been periods marked by commendable Christian lay activity in the social field.

In 120 out of the 167 parishes of Haiti a parochial school is operated by the pastor with a small percentage of the expenses paid by the government. Despite the relatively poor educational record of the nation, a number of clergymen and Catholic leaders have demonstrated praiseworthy devotion to the problem of schools.

Haiti today counts 465 priests or one for each 7,400 faithful, a figure 36% below the continental average of 5,410 faithful per priest. There are 178 Brothers and 701 Sisters.

Protestantism is strong in Haiti, with 327,140 adherents and a personnel of 1,510. One peculiar reason for the growth has been the employment of the creole folk language in Protestant religious services. The Protestant social and educational activities have made impact, as witness Dr. Frank Laubach's campaigns against illiteracy.

HONDURAS
(Republica de Honduras)

Area: 43,280 square miles. *Population:* 2,087,000 (1963)
Capital: Tegucigalpa. *Language:* Spanish

DESCRIPTION Honduras possesses the largest portion of mountain country among the Central American states. It counts the major concentration of its people (77%) in this highland area which occupies the center of its territory. Its long Caribbean coastline measures 500 miles while the coastal segment on the Pacific totals only 40 miles. While it has considerable fertile acreage and rich forests, Honduras' tough terrain has impeded much necessary road building. The result is a number of isolated communities which find it difficult to contact each other or the outside world. Guatemala lies above it, with diminutive El Salvador snuggled between these two countries along the Pacific. Nicaragua lies below it.

POPULATION Honduras has an average density of 45 per square mile. Its rate of population increase in recent years has been reported as 2.7% with a trend toward a higher average in the 1960's. The rural population of Honduras runs to 75%, a percentage which among all Latin American countries is topped only by Guatemala and Haiti.

Indians in Honduras number 125,000 while the mestizo population runs to 1,670,000. Negroes and mulattoes total 55,000. Life expectancy

198

in Honduras is 44 years for men, 46 years for women. The medical care in Honduras provides 2.1 doctors and 20 hospital beds for each 10,000 persons.

Illiteracy in Honduras reaches 64.8% of the population. Of the 315,000 children of primary school age, 205,000, 65%, are in school. Of the 198,000 young people of secondary school age, 15,000, 7.5%, are in school. Honduras has close to the lowest percentage of university students in the Latin American world, though the total has moved up from 1,350 in 1960 to 1,690 in 1963. The government initiated in 1963 a University City in the suburbs of Tegucigalpa and received a grant of $325,000 from the Ford Foundation for laboratory equipment.

SOCIAL AND ECONOMIC FACTORS   The 1961 per capita distribution of national income in Honduras came to $251.70, which was $169 below the Latin American average of $420.70. The total value of exports for that year was $64,300,000. The major export commodity was bananas which represented 46.1% of the sales, while coffee represented 18.9%.

The standard pattern in Latin America of a concentration of agricultural land in a relatively few large properties and an extremely large number of minifundia at the other end of the gamut characterizes the situation in Honduras. Two firms possess holdings totaling 500,000 acres which is 8% of all of the nation's farm land under cultivation. Three-fourths of all the country's farms represent only 16% of the total cultivated area and 10% of all the farms are less than a hectare (approximately two and a half acres) in size. Only 21% of all farms are worked by their owners, which means that the vast bulk are operated by renters, sharecroppers or under other forms of tenure.

In Honduras the housing shortage is grave; so is the water and sewerage situation. Only some 10% of the total population has home water service and 9% has sewerage installations. Hence a high incidence of water-borne diseases in the general mortality rate.

Very promising are the public service enterprises in progress through Alliance for Progress and other assistance funds. In 1963 water supply and sewerage networks to serve over 250,000 persons were under construction.

RELIGION   Evangelization in the area now situated within the territory of Honduras began in approximately 1550. Several Franciscans were martyred there by the Indians in 1612. Between the years 1857 and 1864 the Spaniard Manuel Subirana quickened the spiritual life of the Indians in Honduras by his apostolic activities.

In 1880 a wave of vexatious harassment was visited on the Church by the civil arm and separation of Church and State took place. In

1916 new dioceses were established but several years passed before the government gave practical recognition to the fact.

Today Honduras possesses 154 priests and 71 parishes with an average of 15,000 persons per parish. There are 20 Brothers and 178 Sisters. Besides the shortage of clergy, the wide dispersion of much of the population and a prevalence of common law unions represent special obstacles to the ministry of souls. Religious workers in Honduras note the deep sincerity of faith and the spontaneous religious spirit among the rural populace.

Protestants in Honduras are reported as totaling 34,488, served by 242 Honduran and 157 foreign personnel.

MEXICO
(Estados Unidos Mexicanos)

Area: 760,340 square miles. *Population:* 37,940,000 (1963)
Capital: Mexico City. *Language:* Spanish and local Indian
tongues

DESCRIPTION   While not always ranked with Argentina, Chile and
Uruguay as among the strongest of the Latin American countries,
Mexico deserves such rating in view of its recent outstanding advances.
Since 1950 the Mexican economy has been one of the highest in Latin
America. It has given exceptional attention to education and other
social betterment programs.

Next to Brazil, Mexico is the largest Latin American country in
population. The Sierra Madre mountains on the Pacific side and a
continuation of the Rockies on the Gulf side form the limits of a vast
tableland one mile to 8,000 feet high which possesses a delightful
climate and favorable soil and living conditions. The coastal lowlands
are tropical or subtropical, with heavy rainfall on the Gulf but with
dry areas along the Pacific and in the northern interior which require
irrigation. Mexico has 49 ocean ports and extensive air service with
participation of 58 carrier companies.

POPULATION   The national average density is 46 per square mile. Population increase is 2.9% which, in view of the country's size, presents enormous national problems. Its population is 50% urban, which places it with the half dozen highest ranking Latin American countries in this respect.

Mexico possesses the largest number of persons claiming Indian blood found in any Latin American country, namely, 7,580,000 or 20% of the whole. Its mestizo population is 60%, 22,760,000. It counts 85,000 Negroes and mulattoes.

Despite recent public health improvements Mexico's life expectancy is still the lowest of all Latin America—37.9 years for men and 39.8 for women. Its provision of doctors is fairly good, namely, 5.8 per 10,000 persons, but its hospital beds are percentually few—14 per 10,000 persons.

Illiteracy in Mexico has been reduced from 58% in 1944 to 38% in 1962. Almost three quarters (74.1%) of the children of the primary school age group are in school. Of the 3,916,000 young people of the secondary school age group, 487,000 or 12.4% are in school. University students number 87,000. There are 43 universities or university-level institutions and 35 specialized advanced training schools. Education has risen from 16% to 22% in federal budget allotments.

ECONOMIC AND SOCIAL FACTORS   The per capita distribution of Mexico's national income is practically at the level of the continental average; this over-all average for 1961 was $420.70 while Mexico's was $415.40. There is a spread in Mexico's export trade that keeps the nation from the handicap of dependency on a single commodity. Cotton represented the principal item at 20.68% of the total. Coffee was next at 9.41%; sugar 6.94%.

Long ago Mexico got beyond the talking stage in agrarian reform. In the first 11 months of 1963 it distributed some 2,000,000 hectares (approximately 4,900,000 acres) which, by Mexican records, brought the total since 1915 to more than 50,000,000 hectares (c. 123,500,000 acres).

One of Mexico's major agricultural problems is irrigation. The country has a high percentage of land suitable for agriculture but an estimated 63% must be irrigated. Mexico is already a land of huge irrigation networks; in 1962 nearly 9,000,000 acres, or one third of the total cultivated area, were watered artificially.

Weak points in Mexico are housing facilities, drinking water and sewerage. Two million housing units will be needed by 1970; 130,000 units a year must be built but in 1960 only 60,000 were actually constructed. Preference is given currently to larger towns in the installation of potable water services. Virtually all Mexico City's inhabitants now have sewerage service but barely 40% of the urban population in the provinces is thus accommodated.

RELIGION Among all the Latin American nations, Mexico's religious history is one of the most fascinating.

Padre Juan Diaz in 1518 celebrated the first Mass on soil that is now Mexican. An important group of Franciscans from Ghent reached Mexico in 1522 and in 1524 a similarly distinguished mission band came which included the celebrated Padre Toribio de Benavente Motolinía. Evangelization of the Indians was launched and considerable attention given to Indian policy. This is evident from the protests in 1528 by Bishop Zumarraga, the first ordinary in Mexico, against exploitation of the Indians. In 1537 Pope Paul III issued his bull *Sublimis Deus* in which he declared that Indians, regardless of whether they were Christians or pagans, could not be reduced to slavery.

The epoch-making apparitions of Our Lady of Guadalupe to Juan Diego occurred in December 1531 and began immediately to play their decisive role for the faith in Mexico and the Latin American world.

Many schools were founded in the 16th century aimed at the education of the Indians. In 1538 Bishop Vasco de Quiroga of Michoacán, a former lay administrator distinguished for his social mindedness who answered a delayed vocation to the ministry, founded the first hospitals. In 1541 every parish was asked to establish a school and a hospital. Pedro López founded the first leper asylum in 1564. By 1644 it was possible for the Mexican authorities to notify Philip IV that no further religious need be sent from Spain since the local supply of vocations amply met the needs.

But with the 1700's the Spanish right of patronage became in many ways an instrument of oppression for the Church in the new world and certainly so in Mexico. Though independence came to Spanish America in the early 19th century in Mexico it was 1836 before proper affiliations were established with the Holy See, due to local strife and Spain's opposition in Rome. By 1829 there was no bishop left in Mexico and religion was in a perilous state. By the time the situation was remedied great harm had been done and conditions became progressively worse. The forces leagued with religion and those who spoke for the new Mexico became openly hostile toward each other.

Mexico's constitution of 1857 no longer recognized Catholicism as the official religion. In 1861 when the liberals had won the bloody civil war they declared separation of Church and State. The reforms of 1873-75 decreed nationalization of Church property, civil marriage, civil burial and expulsion of religious. The long regime of "*Profirismo,*" as the years of Diaz were characterized, were bitterly anti-clerical.

The Constitution of Queretaro of 1917 still in force accentuated the repression of Church rights as to ecclesiastical property, public worship, civil and political rights of the clergy. Calles from 1926 to 1929 created a state of open persecution by his laws of 1926, which suspended all worship and sought to create a schism in the clergy. The death before a firing squad of Padre Pro, S.J., has since symbolized the heroic Catholic resistance. New laws in 1934 rendered it impossible for the Church to engage in education. In 1935 every house of worship was "nationalized."

But despite these obstacles, or possibly because of them, the Church in Mexico attained a spiritual vigor which makes it in some respects the strongest in all Latin America. Through the years emphasis has been placed on worship. Pilgrimages have played a notable role. Systematic instruction in Christian doctrine has been pursued through the creation of over 12,000 teaching centers and the enlistment of 35,000 lay teachers. The Christian Family Movement has become important. Vocations have flourished though not to the degree that would provide an adequate clergy. The lay apostolate is very strong.

Meanwhile during the past 20 years an atmosphere of calm has progressively developed. A spirit of tolerance has grown up between the two powers. Application of the hostile legislation has abated though all the laws remain on the books.

In 1961 there were 47 dioceses, 6,903 priests (1 per 4,693 Catholics), 18,423 Sisters, 451,611 children in Catholic schools.

One may suggest that after such hideous hostility to the Church for a period of over a hundred years, surely Catholics must by now represent a mere embattled minority. Not at all; a judicious survey in June 1961 resulted in the conservative estimate that 32,383,000 Mexicans regard themselves as Catholics in a population of approximately 37,000,000.

The Protestant Church in Mexico reported in 1961 a total membership of 897,227. It possesses Mexican personnel to a total of 2,521 and foreign personnel numbering 431.

NICARAGUA
(Republica de Nicaragua)

Area: 57,150 square miles. *Population:* 1,630,000 (1963)
Capital: Managua. *Language:* Spanish

DESCRIPTION Nicaragua is the largest of the five states of Central America. It has Honduras to the north of it and Costa Rica to the South. It possesses a central mountainous region that counts numerous volcanic peaks and two large lakes which figure prominently as means of communication. Two coastal plains border the Caribbean and the Pacific. The Pacific plain represents less than 20% of the national territory but holds over 66% of the population and is of major importance for economic life.

The eastern plain, called the Miskito Coast, does not get its name, as one might suppose, from the notorious hard-biting insect. It comes, rather, from an Indian tribe that has long lived along the 300-mile eastern shoreline bathed by the Caribbean. It is a remote and meager region possessing a labyrinth of lagoons that in the lusty days gone by provided perfect hiding places for pirates.

POPULATION Nicaragua has a density of 26 persons per square mile. Its current rate of population increase is 3%, ranking it among the five fastest growing countries in Latin America. Venezuela matches

Nicaragua in its rate of increase, while Costa Rica, the Dominican Republic and Guatemala have slightly higher rates. Nicaragua's urban population is a moderately low 37%.

Nicaragua's major ethnic group is the mestizos who number 1,220,000 and are 75% of the whole. The Indians total 65,000, 4% of the population, while Negroes and mulattoes count 155,000. Life expectancy of the country's inhabitants is 55 years. Doctors average 3.5 per 10,000 persons and hospital beds number 18 per unit of 10,000.

The nation's illiteracy rate is 61.6%. Of the 266,000 children of primary school age, 153,000 or 57.5% are in school. Young people in secondary school number 10,000, a modest 6% of the 165,000 of the country's corresponding age bracket. University students attending the government's National University and the Central American University founded by the Jesuits in 1960 totaled 2,136 in 1963-64. The government's investment in education increased from 11% of the budget in 1957 to 14.5% in 1961.

SOCIAL AND ECONOMIC FACTORS   Nicaragua's per capita distribution of national income in 1961 came to $288.40, which is $132.30 below the mean continental average of $420.70. The nation's total export trade for 1961 was $62,700,000, 34.35% of which represented coffee sales, 26.25% cotton and 12.35% gold.

Whatever inadequacies may be found in the foreign aid programs of the United States and in the operation of such institutions as the Inter-American Development Bank, they have the great merit of having prompted many Latin American nations to engage in planning programs that account for important advances. Such a country is Nicaragua, which heretofore has not been strongly impelled in this direction. Nicaragua's agrarian reform law is a product of this planning. Its program did not go into effect until May of 1963. A survey made a decade ago revealed that 1.6% of the total rural landowners held 42% of all the cultivated land while 35% of the owners held jointly only 2.3% of the farm land of the nation.

Nicaragua is starting bravely along the long road toward better land distribution, fully aware how difficult it will be to secure results without large funds to compensate the owners of the great estates. The program calls for land settlement, crop diversification, agricultural credit, technical assistance to the newly established small farmers. Other areas of recent planning are low-cost housing, community water supply, sanitation, higher education.

RELIGION   The first evangelization in what is now Nicaragua was initiated in 1522. In 1526 several bands of missionaries arrived, including a group of Dominicans led by Bartolome de las Casas. The Indians were at times hostile, and martyrs were numerous in the late 15th and early 16th centuries. The golden age of Catholic life during the Spanish period was the 18th century, until the expulsion of the Jesuits seriously weakened the apostolic forces.

Nicaragua adopted its constitution in 1826. Catholicism was established as the state religion, but agreements with the Holy See were not reached until 1842. During the bizarre days of 1856 when the American marauder William Walker and his henchmen sought to capture the country, the Catholic bishop played a part in the revolt that drove the filibusterers out.

A troubled period for the Church set in in 1893. Separation of Church and State was instituted and the religious congregations were suppressed. The climax came in 1904 when the bishop and clergy were exiled. Peace followed and with the new constitution all religious institutions were guaranteed freedom of action.

Statistics of 1959 indicate the presence of 213 priests in Nicaragua, one for every 7,192 Catholics. Brothers numbered 98 and Sisters 401. Protestants in Nicaragua totaled 38,000.

PANAMA
(Republica de Panama)

Area: 29,200 square miles. *Population:* 1,160,000 (1963)
Capital: Panama City. *Language:* Spanish

DESCRIPTION Panama in its geographic contours is one of the world's most unusual countries. Since it occupies an isthmus between two continents it is understandably very narrow, running in width from 37 to 110 miles. It has a coastline which in length is out of all proportion to the area of the country. On the Caribbean side it is 477 miles long and on the Pacific side it is 767 miles long, a total of 1,244 miles of shore line. The Darian region, which runs from the Canal Zone south to the Colombian border, is almost entirely uninhabited. North of the Canal Zone it runs to the Costa Rican border.

POPULATION Panama has a national density of 37 persons per square mile, though the bulk of population is concentrated near the Canal. Its population increase is 2.8%. Its urban population is quite strong in that it constitutes 47% of the nation. The mestizo element in the population runs to 60% (690,000). The Indian sector is 70,000, or 6% while its Negroes and mulattoes total 130,000. Life expectancy is reassuringly high, 60.4 years for men and 63.1 years for women.

208

Its service in doctors averages 3.5 for each 10,000 persons and it possesses the unusually high average of 38 hospital beds for each unit of 10,000 persons.

Panama has reduced its illiteracy average from 36% in 1940 to 22% in 1960. Best work in this line was done in the cities, since the rural areas currently have six times more illiterates than the urban areas. The primary schools are training 87% of the children of the corresponding age group while 30% of the age group of the secondary school level are likewise being cared for. Its university students currently total 3,300.

SOCIAL AND ECONOMIC FACTORS   The per capita distribution of the national income averages $371, which is only $49.70 below the continental mean of $420.70. Panama, on the basis of 1960 figures, has the dubious distinction of possessing the lowest export trade total of al the Latin American nations, $19,400,000. Even Paraguay's figure is almost 30% higher. Bananas were by far the major factor in sales, representing 72.89% of the total.

The country of Panama is characterized by the large percentage of its unexploited possessions. Only a quarter of its land suitable for farming and ranching is under cultivation or in pasture. Only a small portion of its forest area renders a return and only 10% of its electric power potential has as yet been utilized.

The country's Agrarian Reform Commission is initiating a program to alter this situation. The problem turns to a lesser degree than in other countries around the uneven distribution of lands and concerns itself more with currently unused or inadequately used areas. The Commission seeks to regularize squatters' lands, to confirm unclear titles and to claim sizable tracts of illegally occupied government lands.

Housing needs of the nation are another basic problem. The current shortage runs to 130,000 units of which 15,000 are needed in Panama City alone. Construction should average 17,500 units a year and present construction is far below this figure. Only 46% of the population now enjoys proper household water connections and only 28% has sewage facilities.

RELIGION   The Church has been present in Panama since 1513 and the Indians of the region early received attention. Nevertheless Panama was always considered primarily as a point of arrival and departure for persons going elsewhere. Its religious houses served as temporary residences for personnel going to or returning from the *audiencia* of Peru. In 1582 the Jesuits set up a school for local service and in 1648 established St. Francis Xavier University, which was closed at the time of the expulsion.

When the struggle for independence began, the Spanish missionaries were expelled and the Church suffered generally. Proper provision for the area was not seriously considered until the 20th century when work began on the canal.

Today there are 71 parishes in half a dozen ecclesiastical territories; 48 of these are proximate to the canal, 7 are in Darien, south of the canal, and 16 in the northern interior. Priests total 163, Brothers 55 and Sisters 328. Vincentian Fathers from the United States have served the Canal Zone from the beginning. The cosmopolitan nature of the neighborhood about the canal has militated against strong family and community life and the interior of the country suffered until recently through general lack of concern for these areas.

Protestants in Panama in 1961 numbered 41,778 served by 327 Panamanians and 255 foreign personnel.

PARAGUAY
(Republica del Paraguay)

Area: 157,050 square miles. *Population:* 1,848,000 (1963)
Capital: Asunción. *Language:* Spanish, Guaraní

DESCRIPTION   While Paraguay is, like Bolivia, a land-locked nation,
it is much better off than Bolivia. Its capital, Asunción, which is 1,000
miles from the sea, has easy river contact with the Atlantic for vessels
up to 12-foot draft. Concepción, its deep inland city, though 1,800
miles from the sea, can be reached by craft which though smaller
are adequate freighters.

Paraguay is approximately the size of California, well served by
rivers; but since it is only thinly populated, it has few roads and only
a few of these are more than bullock paths. Most of its people live
in the eastern third of its territory.

West of the Paraguay River lies the vast area known as the Gran
Chaco which geographers compare to the Ganges Valley in India.
But while the Ganges counts roughly a hundred million inhabitants,
the Chaco is one of the most thinly settled areas in Latin America,
thanks principally to the fact that it is so completely undeveloped.
Argentina, Bolivia and Brazil also hold portions of it and in the 1930's.
Bolivia and Paraguay fought a costly boundary war here.

211

Eastern Paraguay has excellent cattle pasturage and farm lands and luxuriant forests, most of them undeveloped; barely 1% of the country is under cultivation. It is one of the best watered countries in the world. It has a future and is taking steps to overcome its handicaps. With a dictator-type government since 1954, it has not yet found its permanent political formula.

POPULATION   Paraguay, with a density of 11 persons per square mile, is slightly above Bolivia with its density of nine. Population increase is 2%, a low figure in the current Latin American world. The urban population is 35%. The great mass of its people are mestizos who in 1963 counted 1,290,000 or 70%. The declared Indians number 55,400 or 3%. Negroes and mulattoes total 13,000. Life expectancy is 52 years. Doctors number 5.3 per 10,000 persons and hospital beds are a low 8 per 10,000 persons.

Paraguay has succeeded in reducing its illiteracy to 34.2%. Three-fourths of its school age children are enrolled in primary schools, a genuine achievement when it is recognized that 80% of the school buildings are wretched structures. The intermediate schools train 13% of the corresponding age level.

There are two universities, the National and the Catholic. Total enrollment is 3,900, the majority following law and the humanities, a Latin American tradition. In 1962, 760 of the students in the National University were enrolled in law while there were 85 in agricultural engineering, 75 in civil engineering, 7 in industrial engineering. The nation also has four small technical colleges.

SOCIAL AND ECONOMIC FACTORS   Paraguay's per capita distribution of national income is $193.20, which is $227.50 below the mean average of $420.70 representing the per capita of the total Latin American world. Haiti's and Bolivia's per capita are the only ones lower than Paraguay's. The export total for 1961 was $27,000,000. Principal commodity was meat products which represented 26.46% of the total, wool 18.64%, quebracho extracts 10.93%. The quebracho tree possesses very hard wood with special market value while its bark provides tannin, dye and medical products.

Most farming in Paraguay is carried out on small properties concentrated near the capital. The land system includes a high percentage of squatters who work almost one half of the existing farms and 10% of the land in use. The government aims to give them titles and improve their product. It likewise hopes to help them replace their thatch-roofed huts with dirt walls and floors. Barely 25% of Paraguay's urban population and 15% of the total population enjoys a proper water supply. Of the 300,000 dwellers in the capital, 172,000 are served by a water system, the remainder by wells and cisterns. Only one-third of the dwellers in the capital are served by the sewerage system in the capital which is the only sewerage system in all Paraguay.

Most important single factor touching Paraguay's future is the steady increase in its national planning in the social and economic fields, particularly since 1960.

RELIGION Asunción, the present capital of Paraguay, was founded in 1537 and became immediately a base for Indian missions. By far the most celebrated of the mission projects were the Paraguay Reductions established by the Jesuits in the region of the Paraná River. This "Christian Republic" began in 1610 and at its peak in the second quarter of the 1700's possessed 30 highly organized settlements totalling 150,000 inhabitants. By the time of the suppression of the Jesuits by the King of Spain in 1767—157 years later—three-quarters of a million Indians had been under Jesuit care in this enterprise.

The patronage of the Spanish kings, which served religion so well in the early period of the Spanish regime, proved a disservice when independence came to Latin America since both freedom's worthy leaders and the irresponsible adventurers who on occasions grabbed power felt obliged to claim for the sake of their prestige the right of patronage over the Catholic Church in the new republics.

The evil of this is accentuated in Paraguay. The dictator Francia amid all his excesses called himself "Chief of the Church" and took charge of all its property and personnel. Lopez the father and Lopez the son assumed similar roles. When the son was killed at the end of the terrible War of the Triple Alliance, Paraguay possessed only 300,000 survivors out of its former 1,100,000, with a disproportion in the nation of one man to every 28 women. But still the Church was caught in the strife between Paraguay's big families, which lined up either under the banner of the Colorados (Reds), who were anticlerical liberals, or that of the Azules (Blues), who favored Catholic institutions.

Religious peace came with the impact of the Chaco War in 1932. The Church functions today with vigor and its lay organizations prove able leaders and cooperators. The Franciscan Tertiaries, for example, aid the clergy in admirable fashion. There are federations of Catholic doctors, Catholic lawyers, and similar groups as well as Catholic Action units and the Legion of Mary. Radio Caritas, operated by the Franciscans, is quite renowned.

Clergy today number 393, an average of one to 4,700. Brothers number 172 and Sisters 582. Protestants in Paraguay total 36,560.

PERU
(Republica del Peru)

Area: 496,220 square miles. *Population:* 11,600,000 (1963)
Capital: Lima. *Language:* Spanish, Quechua, Aymará

DESCRIPTION   Peru has its face to the Pacific Ocean and its back to
the Amazon Basin where it borders on Brazil. Ecuador is its neighbor
to the north while Bolivia and Chile lie to the south. It is made up
of three major regions: the Coast, the Sierra and the Selva.

The lowland coastal area is one of the most arid deserts of the
world but narrow valleys carry rivers from the Andes to the sea. From
the air these valleys look like rich emerald green ribbons as the river
waters make them blossom. Important cities such as Lima and Callao
are found here, and intensive commercial agriculture flourishes. Thus,
although only 13% of the total area, this region counts 30% of the
nation's population.

The Andean Highlands, or Sierra, include ranges with séven peaks
above 19,000 feet. The intermountain plateaus and valleys are the
home of 60% of Peru's population, though they represent only 27%
of the territory. A large percentage of the inhabitants are of Indian
stock and many speak only local tongues.

The third region, the Selva or forest, represents 60% of Peru's
territory but counts only 10% of the population. It is hot and densely

214

wooded, slanting toward Brazil. It is Peru's relatively unimportant backyard.

POPULATION   Peru has a density of 22 persons per square mile and population-wise is growing at the rate of 2.8% annually. Today 41% of its people are urban dwellers. It is one of the great Indian nations of Latin America since 4,640,000 people, 40% of the nation, declare themselves of Indian stock. Another 32%—3,712,000—are mestizo. There are 150,000 Negroes and mulattoes found for the most part along the coast. Peru's life expectancy average is 46.1 years. Its doctors average 4.7 per 10,000 persons, somewhat less than the mean continental average of 5.5 doctors per 10,000 persons. There are 22 hospital beds per 10,000 persons.

Peru's illiteracy runs to 53%, chiefly among the Indians. In its primary schools are 1,433,000 children, 87.4% of the corresponding age group. Those in secondary school number 202,000, 17.1% of the corresponding age group. University students numbered 37,000 in 1962. As of 1964, public education in Peru was declared free of charge at all levels from primary school through the university.

SOCIAL AND ECONOMIC FACTORS   The per capita distribution of the national income in 1961 was $267.50. This is $153.20 below the mean continental average of $420.70. Peru's total exports in 1960 were $431,500,000. Cotton was the major item, representing 16.92% of the total export value, sugar the second at 11% of the value, and iron ore 7.55% of the value.

The 1962 Agrarian Reform Law amply demonstrates the determination of the Peruvian Government to face up to the nation's land problem. Slightly more than three-quarters of all farm land in Peru is presently held by less than 4,000 owners who average over 9,000 acres each. At the other extreme, 90% of all farms in Peru average less than five acres each.

Peru has another tremendous problem in the shortage, as of 1961, of nearly 2,000,000 dwellings. Important steps have been taken, but the pace of provision has not yet caught up with the requirements. Safe water supply is currently available to only 60% of the urban population and is virtually non-existent in rural areas. Examination of 50,673 medically-certified death records in 1960 attested that over 10% of the deaths were attributed to water-borne diseases. A strong movement is afoot for better sewerage facilities.

RELIGION   Lima, founded in 1535, became during the 16th century the queen city of Spanish South America in all its political, commercial and cultural life. In 1546 it became the official ecclesiastical center as well since it was named the metropolitan for the vast area from Nicaragua to the southernmost point of Spanish penetration. Church and State combined to provide a flourishing creole society. Universities were established at Lima and Charcas. Printing was introduced and in 1560 dictionaries and grammars were prepared of the Indian languages. The First Council of Lima was held in 1583.

The 17th century is regarded as the "religious century." Saint Rose of Lima lived and made her impress, to be canonized eventually in 1671. The Jesuits founded their reductions among the Chiquitos, the plains Indians in what is now the Bolivian lowlands.

The political and economic decadence of the 18th century represented a period of retrogression for Church institutions as well. The monastic life and the religious life generally lost much of its savor. The Indian revolt of Tupac-Amaru in 1780 harmed the morale of all.

In the wars of independence Peru remained among the longest faithful to Spain; the creoles (as American-born Spanish were called) had profited greatly under Spain and feared the Indians. But the victory of Sucre at Ayacucho in 1824 sealed the fate of the Spanish. The 19th century was marked by difficulties for Spanish clergy and the Hispanophiles wherever they remained and for religion as a whole whenever anti-clerical elements appeared in the government. Religion languished.

Lima's Eucharistic Congress of 1934 and the rise of Catholic Action are referred to as factors which played a part in the resurgence of the faith. Today Peru possesses 34 ecclesiastical territories headed by bishops and served by 1,812 clergy, 1,096 Brothers and 3,957 Sisters. Catholic education represents a force while effective movements for vocations are gaining results. The laity play a steadily increasing role in Christian programs.

Notable influence is exercised by Catholic leaders in social reform. In 1962 the Archbishop of Cuzco decreed that rural holdings belonging to the Church under his jurisdiction should be subdivided and sold at half their value to small-scale farmers, payments to be made in modest installments over ten years. Other Church holdings have been similarly made available.

Protestants in Peru in 1961 numbered 94,053, served by 842 Peruvian and 733 foreign personnel.

URUGUAY
(Republica Oriental
del Uruguay)

Area: 72,172 square miles. *Population:* 2,590,000 (1963)
Capital: Montevideo. *Language:* Spanish

DESCRIPTION   Uruguay is a country of rolling grassy plains and gentle
contours, so constituted that its hardy populace has been able to
place 88% of all available land under cultivation or in pasture. Brazil
is its northern neighbor and Argentina lies below it, separated to the
west by the Uruguay River. The country is the size of North Dakota,
the smallest republic in South America. It boasts of being the best
planned and best conducted state in the Latin American world, a
pioneer in organizing a full-scale modern social welfare program.

POPULATION   Uruguay has a national average of 39 persons per square
mile. It has the lowest population growth rate of all Latin American
nations, nine-tenths of one per cent. Perhaps the reason for this is
found in its percentage of urban dwellers, who total 81%, the highest
in Latin America. The great mass of its population is unmixed European stock. It has no Indians, a total of 100,000 mestizos and 60,000
Negroes and mulattoes. Its life expectancy average is 64 years for
men and 66 for women. Its percentage of doctors is high, 11.3 for
each 10,000, which compares very favorably with mean continental

average of 5.5 doctors per 10,000 persons. It has 39 hospital beds per 10,000 persons.

Uruguay's illiterates represent 15% of the population, the lowest rate in Latin America except for Argentina's which is 13.6%. Its primary schools are training 97.8% of all the children of the corresponding age bracket and its secondary schools count 31.8% of all young people of the similarly corresponding age bracket. University students number 16,000.

ECONOMIC AND SOCIAL FACTORS   The per capita distribution of the income in 1961 was $560.90, which is $140.20 above the mean continental average of $420.70. The value of Uruguay's total exports for 1960 ran to $129,500,000. All of its major commodities pertained to its grazing industry; the top item was wool which represented 34.88%, next came meat products, 23.79%, and then hides, 6.13%.

In Uruguay the cattle man has always been supreme, to the degree that technical diagnosis establishes that today the nation is being hurt through improper attention to agriculture. It is unlikely that more capital can be attracted for agriculture until the conditions that induce low productivity can be overcome.

The problem of migration to urban centers is not at all as acute in Uruguay as in other Latin American countries. This, along with its low record of population growth and its relatively high economic strength throughout the private sector, accounts for its relatively small housing crisis compared with other Latin American nations. Nevertheless there was a shortage in 1963 of some 100,000 housing units.

In countries such as Uruguay which possess more mature social development, it is interesting to note that there is the same evidence of stepped-up national planning as in other Latin American lands. However, such planning is on a different level than in countries where national programs are still in their earlier phases.

RELIGION   Uruguay like Argentina long suffered from the fact that Spain did all its thinking so far as South America was concerned in terms of the portage route across the Isthmus of Panama. This meant the entry into the La Plata River country via Peru. By this route Asuncion, Paraguay, was more convenient to the Spaniards than were the areas that now constitute Argentina and Uruguay.

A change came in the early 1600's when Hernando Arias released into the open range of what is now Uruguay 100 head of cattle and 100 horses that he had brought from Spain but that he found he could not transport to Peru via the La Plata River country. This circumstantial act altered the status of the entire southeastern coast of South

America; this livestock flourished marvelously and became the basis for an enormous industry.

The Church had established a foothold in this area early in the 17th century. Franciscan and Jesuit missionaries were found there in 1616. Brother Bernardino de Guzmán founded Soriano in 1620 as the first settlement in the area and converted some of the Indians in the neighborhood. In 1726 a parish was established in Montevideo and was made subject to Buenos Aires. The first bishop in Uruguay was named in 1856 and several dioceses were created in 1897.

Current Church history began in 1903 with the rise to power of Uruguay's great statesman, José Batlle y Ordóñez. Batlle accomplished much for the country, particularly in social legislation, but unfortunately was an apostle of the positivism of Auguste Comte to the degree that he saw no role for the Church in public life. In 1916 separation of Church and State took place, a step readily acceptable to ecclesiastical authorities were it not for the veiled persecution that prevailed. The laws of secularization that were imposed were quite stringent. Today the spirit of laicism and the agnostic philosophy advanced in educational circles are very pronounced.

On the favorable side, Uruguay possesses a small but excellent clergy and a lay elite of outstanding quality. Despite financial problems, there is a steady increase in Catholic educational services and in the social apostolate. Priests total 686 or one for each 3,775 citizens. The 162 parishes of the nation average 13,000 members each. Brothers number 741 and Sisters 1,775.

The Protestant population of Uruguay totals 42,594, served by a staff of 247 of whom 167 are Uruguayans.

VENEZUELA
(Republica de Venezuela)

Area: 352,143 square miles. *Population:* 8,391,000 (1963)
Capital: Caracas. *Language:* Spanish

DESCRIPTION   Venezuela possesses a coastline of 1,750 miles along
the Caribbean Sea with a string of 72 islands off its shore. Colombia
lies to the west and British Guiana to the east. It has Brazil for a neighbor on its southern border. The majority of Venezuela's people live
in the Andean highlands which occupy a minor portion of the nation's
territory. After stretching northward from the southern tip of the
South American continent they come to an end on the edge of the
Orinoco Valley.

The Orinoco is South America's second largest river system, smaller
only than the Amazon. The system drains almost four-fifths of
Venezuela. Venezuela is a land of extreme contrasts, as one recognizes
by comparing Caracas, the brilliant capital, with the vast southern
hinterland of lonely plains which geographically belong to the Amazon
Valley. Eastern Venezuela includes 59% of the nation's territory and
20% of its population.

In the low coastal area, Lake Maracaibo has since 1917 become the
great focal point; here today is found the greatest oil field in Latin
America. In 1960 production ran to almost three million barrels a day.

Foreign interests, including American companies, work the wells and pay 60% of the revenues to Venezuela.

POPULATION Venezuela's national average density is 19 persons per square mile. Annual population increase is 3%. The urban population represents 61% of the total. Indians represent 2% of the nation, or 167,000, while the mestizos total 30%, or 2,517,000.

Negroes and mulattoes number 2,670,000, thus making Venezuela a major nation for Negro-mulatto population. Brazil ranks first in this respect, Colombia second and Venezuela third. Apart from those in Brazil, the heavy Negro-mulatto concentration follows the Caribbean and Pacific coastal areas from Venezuela into Ecuador. Of the 20 Latin American nations, 16 report Negroes and mulattoes, with a Latin American total approaching 30,000,000.

Venezuela's life expectancy rate is 52.8 years. Doctors average 7 per 10,000 persons and hospital beds average 36 per 10,000 persons.

The illiteracy rate for the nation is 47.8%. Primary school attendance, recently much improved, represents 88.3% of the children who comprise the corresponding age group. The young people in secondary school number 19.6% of the total comprising the similarly corresponding age group. Venezuela's university students in 1960 numbered 24,900. The new Andrés Bello University conducted by the Church gives great promise.

Venezuela possesses a National Institute for Education Cooperation directed by representatives of management, labor and the government for improving professional training for workers. For its financing, 80% of the funds come from business and the workers, 20% from the government. In 1962, 13,000 students were registered.

SOCIAL AND ECONOMIC FACTORS The 1961 per capita distribution of Venezuela's national income gives us the figure of $644.50, which is $223.80 above the continental average of $420.70. This makes the country second only to Argentina which reported a per capita of $799.00.

Venezuela's foreign trade record for 1960 was $2,518,000,000 which is practically twice as high as Brazil's and thus far and away the highest among all Latin American nations. As can well be understood, 90.55% of this is foreign petroleum revenues. The second most important commodity is iron ore, rating 6.8%. Coffee, which by the standards of many other nations represents heavy sales, meant only 0.89% of Venezuela's foreign trade.

Much has been done in recent years to better the Venezuelan agrarian structure, housing, rural water supply, access roads, agricultural credit and extension. Because of rapid growth as well as inadequate distribution of land and insufficient farming methods, Venezuela for a number of years was importing as much as one third of its food supplies at a cost of some $200,000,000 a year. In 1962 this had been reduced to 15% of the total food needs and the government is working toward further reductions.

Among Latin American countries, Venezuela rates high in the dimensions of its land expropriation and redistribution program. By the end of 1963 nearly 60,000 rural families had been established in 650 settlements by the National Agrarian Institute. These families took possession of approximately 4,000,000 acres of land. To set them up the government spent $130,000,000.

Among private colonization efforts, one that has started well is operated by the Catholic Charities organization of Venezuela. Its first settlement is a few miles from the city of Maturín. Here 100 rural families will live and work on an area of 750 acres.

RELIGION   The first bishop in Venezuela was named for the see of Coro in 1532. In 1637 Caracas became a see. In 1810 independence reached Venezuela and in 1811 formal liberation was established. The Church through Archbishop Coll y Prat recognized the independence of the country. Bolívar in reply assured the Church of his collaboration.

Later in the century troubles came for the Church. In 1870 the dictator Guzmán Blanco restricted the authority of the archbishop and imposed restrictions on the clergy. By 1872 the seminaries were closed and the courses in ecclesiastical training transferred to the university while the convents were confiscated. By 1874 the religious were expelled, civil marriage was legislated and the governor sought to name a new bishop. By 1888 a tenuous peace was restored.

Today Venezuela possesses 20 ecclesiastical territories with 1,264 priests. Thus there is one priest for each 6,600 citizens. Brothers number 1,127 and Sisters 3,076. The population averages 17,500 per parish. Lay leadership has demonstrated vigor and outstanding ability in conducting such organizations as *Obra de Proteccion al Nino* and *Fe y Alegria* which, though Jesuit founded, has been developed by a lay board of directors.

DISCUSSION OUTLINE

prepared by

V<small>AILE</small> S<small>COTT</small>
Executive Director
Catholic Adult Education Center
Archdiocese of Chicago

General Note

According to the time available and the preparation of the group, preliminary sessions are recommended during which the group may familiarize itself with the social and religious data touching Latin America in general and the individual Latin American nations, as found in the Supplement beginning on page 159.

CHAPTER I

LESSONS OF YESTERDAY FOR
THE NEW LATIN AMERICA

1. How does Bishop McGrath account for the fact that North and Latin America have been strangers to one another?
2. If friendship with Latin America is to be genuine and helpful, what suggestions does the Bishop make? Can you give an example?
3. Discuss Bishop McGrath's remarks concerning the Church's mission today in light of the Second Vatican Council.
4. What can we learn by studying the various changes which have occurred in the Church from one historical period to another?
5. Many people predict that the new Latin America will abandon her Christian past in favor of Communism or agnosticism. Do you agree? What are the alternatives?

CHAPTER II

PLAGUES THAT FOLLOWED FREEDOM

1. Trace the effect of the French Revolution on the Church in Spain and Latin America.
2. What are some of the advantages and disadvantages of the separation of Church and State?
3. What is laicism?
4. What can we learn from the Latin American experience concerning the involvement of the Church in politics?
5. Explain why it is important that the Church be identified as the champion of social justice.

Chapter III

THE GREAT RESURGENCE IN TODAY'S LATIN AMERICA

1. What is the characteristic of the new Latin American role? Explain.
2. Discuss the meaning of a pluralistic society.
3. Why does cultural pluralism require a more personal commitment to the faith?
4. What changes in technique are involved in the policy of "limited objectives" which has been adopted by the Church in Latin America?
5. Discuss the sense of hope for the Church in Latin America.
6. How important is the layman's role in the new Church in Latin America?
7. Why is the Spirit in the Church in Latin America a challenge to Catholics in North America?

Chapter IV

THE CHURCH GOES INTO THE MARKETPLACE

1. Discuss the meaning of the Scripture passages Monsignor Gremillion puts into juxtaposition in his opening remarks.
2. What is the mission of the Church in the temporal order? Do you think we clearly understand the implication of this mission?
3. Monsignor Gremillion speaks of two types of apostolate to the temporal order. Describe how they differ.
4. Why is the Church likely to play a larger role in the social reforms of Latin America than it has in the United States?
5. Emphasis has been placed on the term "continental" in

speaking of social reform in Latin America. Why is this idea stressed?

6. What are some of the organizations North Americans have formed to assist Latin America? Can you describe their particular motivation and purpose?

CHAPTER V

LATIN AMERICA'S PLEA FOR VAST SOCIAL CHANGE

1. One of the early passages in this chapter states that "churchmen throughout the continent . . . favor a true revolution (without violence)." Do you think it is significant that the word "revolution" instead of "evolution" is used? Why?
2. What are the most important economic problems frequently mentioned in the various bishops' statements?
3. In what respect are the social and economic problems of Latin America different from the problems we face in the United States?
4. Do you think that Marxism is more likely to attract followers in Latin America than in the United States? Why?

CHAPTER VI

THE MASTER PLAN ARRIVES IN LATIN AMERICA

1. What are the advantages of the pastoral plans described in this chapter?
2. Discuss the difference between the coordination of the different sectors of action and the integration of these forms of action.
3. What do you think is the most significant quality of Bishop Eugenio of Brazil?

4. Do you think that pastoral plans are as necessary in North America as in Latin America?

5. What are some of the things that Catholics in North America and Europe can do to help the Latin American Episcopacy with pastoral planning?

CHAPTER VII

CATHOLIC SCHOOLS AND A STUDY ON BASIC EDUCATION

1. (a) What do you think of the idea of putting a good religious instruction program into the public school systems of Latin America, where it is legally possible?

   (b) Why has this program not been achieved in the past?

   (c) Discuss whether you think this plan for the religious education of children should replace the effort to build Catholic schools in Latin America.

2. After reading the sections of this chapter, "Measuring Latin American Education through Latin America's Outlay for Education," what conclusions can you come to regarding the problems facing Latin America's educational task?

3. (a) Do you agree with Dr. Betancur that "Education is the soundest cure for poverty, discontent, and every form of violent social revolution"?

   (b) As men become more aware of their deprivation, won't they become even more discontent with their status?

4. What are some of the deficiencies in Catholic education in Latin America which are cited in the quotations from the CIEC report?

5. What is the unique contribution Catholic agencies have made in the field of basic education?

6. Describe the social situation which the basic education movement (M.E.B.) in Brazil is attempting to meet. Discuss its objectives.

CHAPTER VIII

CONFRONTATION OF FAMILIES NORTH AND SOUTH

1. In view of the emphasis placed upon the need for massive social welfare programs and highly organized governmental action to bring about social reform in Latin America, how do you evaluate the potential effectiveness of the Christian Family Movement?
2. Discuss the value of a personal, small-group approach in helping to solve the problems facing Latin America.
3. Can middle-class families in Latin America hope to influence families from the lower economic classes?
4. Discuss the series of vicious circles which Señor Alvarez describes.
5. How does family life in Latin America compare with family life in the United States?

CHAPTER IX

DR. CALVANI AND THE LATIN AMERICAN APOSTOLATE

1. How do you account for the fact that the Church seemed not to have profited from the experience of Father Ricci in China in 1583 and Robert d'Nobili in India in 1623?
2. Discuss the importance of attitude toward Latin America, as it is presented by Dr. Calvani.
3. How would you account for Pope John XXIII's tremendous interest in the future of the Church in Latin America?
4. What is the three-fold obligation of the Church in the United States for Latin America? Do you think we are meeting these obligations?
5. What judgment would you make regarding Cardinal Cushing's point that probably 90% of all the energy and money expended by Catholics for the support of their Church is

devoted to the preservation of the faith in their own parish or diocese, in view of the needs of Latin America?

6. Should our major concern in Latin America be to prevent a Communist take-over?

CHAPTER X

SO YOU THINK YOU'RE READY TO WORK IN LATIN AMERICA!

1. Father Leo Mahon states that our charity, to be effective in vitalizing the Church in Latin America, must be relevant and responsible. In his analysis he summarizes ten points for our consideration. Describe each of these directives in depth. What is your reaction to his ideas?
2. Do you think Father Mahon makes a fair appraisal of the difficulties of North American Catholics?
   How do North American Catholics compare with Latin American Catholics in Father Mahon's terms?
3. Discuss the observations Father Mahon makes regarding the practice of the faith among middle-class Catholics as compared with the lower classes and among intellectuals.
4. Have you ever had an experience similar to Father Mahon's where your value system was questioned? How did you respond?
5. Discuss the four characteristics necessary to make the Christian message relevant to Latin American life.

CHAPTER XI

THE NEW LAITY—SOUTH AND NORTH

1. What is meant by the term "The New Laity"?
2. How would you answer the question "How can I be a Christian in my job?"

3. In what sense does the future of Latin America depend upon the laity?
4. Discuss the three needs which Dr. Calvani thinks that laymen must have to enable them to meet their responsibilities.
5. Describe the purpose of the Papal Volunteers. What is your opinion of the program?
6. Is there a Papal Volunteer program in your diocese? Are you familiar with its activities? Do you participate in its work?

CHAPTER XII

METHODS FOR THE MILLIONS—A WORKING PLAN
TOWARD UNDERSTANDING

1. Evaluate the statement that "The zeal of the apostle is . . . to be subordinated to tactics."
2. What are the aims and goals of CICOP?
3. Do you think that CICOP is designed to meet its projected aims and goals?
4. How would you account for the apathy and indifference shown by North Americans toward Latin Americans?
5. Whose responsibility is it to inform the North American people about Latin America?
6. Discuss the program proposed by Father Nevins for the general media of communication, the press and education.

Index